Praise for Martin Yate's
Keeping the Best . . .

"*Keeping the Best* is an excellent manual for managers searching for a way to make their workgroup more humane and productive—while holding on to those precious people who bring excellence to their companies."

—Kenneth Blanchard, Ph.D.
Co-Author, *The One Minute Manager*

"Excellent; full of practical, down-to-earth techniques."

—Mark Iorio
Manager, Headquarters Human Resources
Honeywell-Bull

"The only businessperson who won't benefit immediately from reading *Keeping the Best* is the owner of a one-person business who wants to stay that way."

—Craig S. Rice
Former President, Royal Crown Cola, Ltd., Canada

"I've always said, it's not the people you fire who make your life miserable . . . it's the people you don't fire! Here's a top-flight guide for every manager about how to keep the best so you don't have to fire the worst!"

—Harvey Mackay
Author, *Swim with the Sharks without Being Eaten Alive*
and *Beware the Naked Man Who Offers You His Shirt*

"*Keeping The Best* has a 'real world' feel; it's the best book on day-to-day management I've ever read."

—Glenn KnicKrehm
President, Bay Resources Corporation

"Too many companies in America—unlike their Japanese and European counterparts—are woefully inadequate when it comes to motivating, retaining, and generally supporting their people. *Keeping The Best* is the book that will help us bridge the gap."

—Mike Badgett
President, Strategic Human Resources, Inc.

"Entrepreneurs instinctively know the talent surrounding them is what makes a difference in their success; to be good is not enough when you're building something that is going to be great. Yate thinks like an entrepreneur!"

—Joseph Mancuso
Founder, The Center for Entrepreneurial Management
and The Chief Executive Officer's Club

"A user-friendly approach: sensible, honest, practical advice."

—Ken Meyer
Vice President of Human Resources
Viacom International

"If every manager in the country read *Keeping The Best*, we headhunters would be out of business."

—Michael Zarnek
President, First Search, Inc.

Keeping the Best

And Other Thoughts on Building a Super Competitive Workforce

Keeping the Best

And Other Thoughts
on Building a Super
Competitive Workforce

Martin Yate

BOB ADAMS, INC.
PUBLISHERS
Holbrook, Massachusetts

Also by Martin Yate:

Hiring the Best: How to Staff Your Department Right the First Time

Knock 'em Dead with Great Answers to Tough Interview Questions

Resumes that Knock 'em Dead

The above titles are available at your local bookstore. If you cannot find them at your local bookstore, you may order them by contacting the publisher at 1-800-872-5627 (617/767-8100 in Massachusetts). Please check your local bookstore first.

ISBN: 1-55850-863-5

Published by Bob Adams, Inc.
260 Center Street
Holbrook, Massachusetts 02343

Manufactured in the United States of America.

A   B   C   D   E   F   G   H   I   J

Every effort has been made to provide accurate and nondiscriminatory information in this book, but it is not intended to be a legal resource. As with all issues concerning the hiring and/or dismissal of employees, consult an attorney if you have any doubts about the legitimacy or legal ramifications of the use of a question or technique in this book in your company, industry, or state. The publisher assumes no liability for damages direct or incidental related to the individual hiring or dismissal decisions of any reader of this book.
—The Publisher

This publication is designed to provide accurate and authoritative information with regard to the subject matter covered. It is sold with the understanding that the publisher is not engaged in rendering legal, accounting, or other professional advice. If legal advice or other expert assistance is required, the services of a competent professional person should be sought.
—From a Declaration of Principles *jointly adopted by a Committee of the American Bar Association and a Committee of Publishers and Associations*

Acknowledgments

Grateful thanks go to: Brandon Toropov, editor of editors, and Bob Adams, my publisher, both of whom labored hard and long over a period of three years to make this book a reality; Carole Richman of Monad Trainer's Aide New York; Lennie Copeland and Lewis Griggs, the San Francisco-based cultural diversity gurus; Christopher Ciaschini for his tireless production work; and Melissa Louer of Albany for sponsoring my first *Keeping the Best* seminar as a work-in-progress.

Contents

Chapter One

❧

The Last
Request

A FRENCHMAN, A JAPANESE, AND AN AMERICAN ALL faced death by a firing squad. Each was granted a last request. After some thought, the Frenchman called for a shot of fine cognac. The Japanese, for his part, asked for one last management lecture. Hearing this, the American groaned and made his own request: "Please—shoot me first. I can't bear another treatise on management techniques."

I'm going to guess that you identify with that story. And it probably won't surprise you to learn that such attitudes are shared by your fellow managers. What you may find surprising is that the very boredom we often feel with the dry and tedious management techniques of the past can actually work to our advantage: we will abandon them all the more quickly. In the end, it's something of a blessing that we have grown so tired of the old approaches. We must find something new in a hurry, something that works.

Managing people, after all, is paramount: it underlies (or should underlie, at any rate) everything else we do. All the strategies, lectures, flow charts, and complicated theories in the world won't help us if the people we're supposed to manage— our employees—are about to leave us for the competition, or if those who remain lack the tools and will to rise above mediocrity. Too often, these problems are exactly what we face. Our job is to find a way out of the downward spiral.

THREE PRINCIPLES

I make no apologies for the fact that this book is not a complicated one. Indeed, all of *Keeping the Best* is founded on three simple principles—principles that are easy enough to grasp initially, but that carry immense implications and can radically change the way we manage our organizations. The principles are these:

One: *The most valuable capital is human capital; the most powerful technology is people.*

Two: *A manager's success is wholly dependent upon his ability to empower others to achieve his goals.*

Three: *Great work occurs only when managers and workers share each other's visions of the present and the future.*

THE MOST IMPORTANT
STRATEGIC FUNCTION FOR THE '90s

We must dramatically increase the consideration, effort, energy, and time that we give to managing our work force.

No longer can the management of human resources be relegated to the status of a "support function" assigned to a few lonely staffers. Rather, managing human resources must become the most important strategic function of every manager in the organization, a long-term, integral consideration behind every action management takes. This is the only way we can build a super-competitive work force: the work force we need to stay in the game in the last decade of the twentieth century.

Indeed, without a responsive, top-notch work force, it is impossible for a manager to fully execute and sustain any other strategic or competitive plan. Without your people enthusiastically supporting your goals, your plan is likely to remain just that: a plan, and not a reality.

We cannot afford the luxury of imagining our employees to be ambulatory pieces of equipment we can plug into place in order to achieve a certain level of profitability. Today, employees at all levels expect to be treated as people first and employees second. They want to know why they should do a particular task; they want to be listened to, and, more significant, they want to be heard. And why shouldn't they? If we won't treat our employees the way they expect to be treated, then we shouldn't be surprised when many of our better people leave us for the competition.

But we don't just want our employees to be "satisfied enough" with our polices to keep them from abandoning us—we want them to take the action necessary to perform at a spectacular level! We want whole-hearted commitment, enthusiasm, and, yes, devotion, and we want it all day long, every working day.

Without committed, enthusiastic, devoted employees, an organization will never perform to its full potential. This applies without exception to every strategic function, and to every area of activity in our organizations. Take customer service, for instance, currently one of the hottest buzzwords in management circles. Corporations around the world are making customer service a top priority, training employees at all levels to "respond to," "cater to," and generally do whatever it takes to "get close to" the customer. But if the employee feels anything less than total commitment, enthusiasm, and devotion to the company, how can we expect him to show total commitment, enthusiasm, and devotion to the customer?

In short, how can we expect the employee to treat customers any better than we treat him? (And our scenario can get even worse: there's always the possibility that a salesperson, for instance, can succeed in getting close to a customer only to leave us for the competition—and might well take that customer with him.)

The same principle holds true for every function in every organization that is not a one-man show. There, and only there, can one rely on the work force being 100% in tune with management goals at all times. For the rest of us, the rule is that we get what we give, whether the work in question is being done for us in our capacity as head of the accounting department, city editor, loading dock foreman, or chairman of the board. In the end, the question we must constantly ask ourselves is this: how can we expect our employees to perform superbly for us if we don't perform superbly for them?

We must develop workers who see company goals and personal goals as different sides of the same coin, or we will never have a super-competitive work force. Of course, we may focus only on the most obvious symptoms of that loss: unenthusiastic lip-service at monthly meetings, mysteriously long lunches, slipped schedules, poor quality, angry customers. The underlying cause of such problems, however, will be the same: our alienation of employees.

It doesn't have to be that way. We find ourselves at a crossroads, at the beginning of a new management journey that can enrich our companies and our lives. It will not be an easy trip, but the rewards will justify the occasional pain of our new approach.

After all, there is no growth, no metamorphosis without pain. And make no mistake: for most of us, what is at issue is nothing less than the complete transformation of our management focus. The changes we must make will be difficult at times, and they may provoke opposition. But they must nevertheless be made if we are to achieve or retain competitiveness in the '90s and beyond.

Can you expect results instantly, within, say, a week or two of implementing the new ideas? No. Old ways die hard. It will take some time—perhaps a great deal of time—to turn the corner and begin building a truly motivated, unstoppable work force. The task ahead is more complicated than simply raising salaries and benefits—money, as discussed later, is only one small part of winning an employee's loyalty. The process is a demanding one that requires consistent, careful work on the part of all individual managers throughout the company. Unfortunately, there is no "quick fix" that will yield a super-competitive work force.

If you are interested only in short-term goals and achievements, then this is not the book for you. If, however, you want to learn how to institute long-term changes that will lead to dramatic and sustainable improvements in your most important strategic resource—your work force—then read on!

Chapter Two

৵

Why People
Leave

REMEMBER ME?

I'm the person who sat patiently for years while you refused to recognize my existence.

I'm the person who loyally gave you the majority of my waking hours, fifty weeks a year. And in return you took my self-respect and dignity. The only time you noticed my presence was when it was time to criticize.

I'm the person who after fifty weeks of tireless and above-average effort each year—effort I made because I believed in you and the company—got my review four weeks late and received a raise exactly the same as the worst performer in my department.

Yes, you might say I'm the salt of the earth. A tower of strength. The kind of employee any company would be proud to employ.

But do you know what else I am?

I am the person who will never come back to work for you. By the way, it does amuse me to see you spending thousands of dollars every year to get me back, when you had me there in the first place. To think that all you had to do was listen to me once in a while, show me a little respect, a little appreciation. But you didn't. Anyway, I wish you all the luck in the world.

HUMAN CAPITAL, PEOPLE TECHNOLOGY

The most valuable capital is human capital; the most powerful technology is people.

We have been misled badly on this score. We have come to believe that a "profitable" business achieves success when it has stacked up some numbingly high pile of dollar bills somewhere. Actually, the firm has only achieved an illusory success; those dollars are only as effective as the people entrusted with their care. And make no mistake: all your employees are entrusted with the care of some form of company resource, if only the money you pay them.

Profits may measure where your company has been in the past; your people determine the future. We can earn no store of resources so vast as to be immune to employee incompetence and alienation. And there is, by the same token, no store of resources so small that a measure of success cannot be achieved with it, given the efforts of a supremely motivated work force.

It follows, then, that the assets we keep in the bank pale to insignificance when compared with the awesome power—potentially creative or potentially destructive—inherent in the assets who sit around the company cafeteria each morning before the day's work begins.

Our technology is often viewed with a similarly alarming lack of perspective. We fooled ourselves into thinking that the dazzling array of miracles our machinery puts at our disposal somehow entitles us to success in our business. But we have yet to come up with a computer terminal, assembly line, or oil supertanker that does not have as its most important component the person deciding when, whether, and how to use it. When it comes time for us to hire, train, or supervise that person, we often treat the task as an annoying technicality—and not as the pivotal and crucial matter it is.

Our attitudes about employment concerns must change, if only for our own survival. To keep the best, management must become equally pro-profits and pro-people. What's more, this must be a matter of personal commitment before we can expect it to emerge as company policy: it is always personal commitment that ultimately engenders formulation and reformulation of company guidelines.

Throughout the last decade, managers have sought to emphasize the worthy goals of getting close to the customer and achieving preeminent quality. Unfortunately, these objectives were often interpreted in such a way as to ignore the basic credo that *you don't get satisfied customers without first having satisfied employees.*

The idea of a competent and committed work force demands more than our lip service. It is time to accept that the people who work for us won't become committed just because we say it's a good thing for them to do.

We must start thinking first and foremost in terms of the prime customer base common to every single enterprise in business today: employees. For without the horses in harness and willing, we will never achieve the other goals we set for our organizations.

These points, too often, have been lost on us. We were somehow fooled into seeing our people themselves as technicalities, not as invaluable partners worthy in their own right of being developed to their highest potential. We considered our subordinates incidental to the reality of the revenue they generated for us. We made a bigger fuss over the new machine than we did over the person we wanted to operate it. And our employees, who weren't stupid, began to notice.

&a   &a   &a

Over forty years ago, playwright Arthur Miller wrote *Death of a Salesman,* a searing drama that told the story of one Willy Loman, summarily fired after two decades of loyalty to his employer. Willy, stripped of his job, also lost his sense of purpose and self. The interesting thing is, if a playwright tried to write that play today, in a contemporary setting, he'd have a hard time of it. Audiences might very well read the synopsis—naive employee puts in his years as a salesperson at one company and gets the shaft—and settle into their seats expecting some type of surrealistic farce. After all, who would put in twenty years these days on some rinky-dink sales job? A chump, that's who. A clown. Get ready for the laughs.

EMPLOYEES LIKE WILLY LOMAN
REALLY ARE DEAD. OR HADN'T YOU HEARD?

For the majority of workers the concept of loyalty itself is dead, too. They have been told time and time again, in deed if not in word, that a company has exclusive loyalty to the bottom right-hand corner of the quarterly profit-and-loss statement. And they've taken that example to heart and done their very best to emulate us—by leaving in droves and, in effect, firing us.

That, as it turns out, is really what we're dealing with. When an employee quits, it means he has just fired you. He is essentially saying, "Look; I've examined this long and hard. To be quite frank about it, you just haven't lived up to my expectations: I'm afraid I'm going to have to cut you loose. To go on like this would be a real mistake for both of us, like trying to fit a square peg in a round hole. I know this might hurt a little now, but in the long run, I think you'll agree that it's for the best. So OK; I'm gone as of Monday." And it's happening with greater and greater frequency.

Just fifteen years ago, managers considered five years on each job to be the minimum indication of a stable work history. Today, such a standard is useless, as anyone working in personnel can attest. The modern employee, however much we might like to deny it, is much more susceptible to wanderlust than his forebears.

If he hears about a new opportunity, he interviews for it first and thinks later about whether it's worth leaving his job with us.

He keeps his resume on a computer disk and updates it monthly, whether or not he's actually on the lookout for a new job. And he thinks nothing of moving on to new challenges, with a new company, when it is convenient for him to do so. Loyalty? How quaint!

This change in outlook couldn't have come at a worse time. Since 1987, according to the Bureau of Labor Statistics, more people have been leaving the work force every year than entering it. New jobs are being created at the rate of three to four million a year, yet on that same yearly basis we are only getting about 1.5 million new workers entering the work force. Consequently, some authorities are estimating that by 1992 there could be two million more jobs than there are people to fill them.

Mark de Michelle, President of the Arizona Public Service Utility, puts it bluntly: "(We anticipate) competing more aggressively than ever before for an ever shrinking labor pool, especially for the more sophisticated worker we are all after in the '90s." While the job market for any given field of specialty, of course, will still have its ups and downs, the overall picture is clear and sobering. In the final decade of the twentieth century, there is no room for complacency or smugness when it comes to the retention of our employees, each of whom represents a significant investment in terms of time, salary, and training. If we are not careful, we are in grave danger of watching helplessly as that investment walks out the door.

Changing the focus

What is required is a radical change in our thinking, a completely new approach to dealing with those who make up our company. We must abandon forever, for instance, the "foreman" school of management techniques, the body of thought that simplifies things so attractively by allowing us to focus only on negative employee behavior. If only management were so simple! If only superior results could actually be delivered by attending solely to such issues as what to do if employees are late, absent, sick, or in violation of some obscure company policy!

Although some management theorists object to parent/child analogies in the workplace, there is no getting around the direct parallel between the parent and the manager as authority figure in the workplace—at least from the employee's point of view. And from the employee's point of view, it is easy to understand how a management style that focuses on creating systems and procedures designed to cudgel minimum productivity out of people, one that focuses exclusively on catching workers who step over the line, does nothing but teach them how not to get caught.

We must recognize excellence of all levels, focusing on the people who aren't tardy or absent, who do follow procedure, who are safe, who do make a contribution—however small. We must also avoid the temptation to champion only those individuals we consider "heros," although this was quite fashionable over the past decade. It is high time that we broaden our own awareness enough to recognize that such an approach, ignoring as it does the importance of team strength and spirit, is fraught with perils. Akio Morita, head of Sony International, puts it this way:

> The U.S. approach is to concentrate on the person who can hit the home run, the very special employee who is obviously destined for great things, the one who is clearly above his peers; the one who can be expected to regularly hit the home run, perhaps even every time at bat. The Japanese approach, on the other hand, is to nurture the people who can bunt and place a single, the ones who give breadth and depth to a whole team.

It gives one pause for thought to see such a telling analogy issued by someone from the other side of the world—but then their baseball is improving.

WHY THEY LEAVE

What prompts an employee's decision to head for the exit? Indications are that a worker's early years on the job are key. A study done recently at Corning Glass, for instance, showed that employees were most likely to leave in their first seven years with the company, and that after this time the likelihood of voluntary departure dropped dramatically. As one might expect, employee pay scales over the periods served highlighted at least one reason: money.

But salary is rarely if ever the only factor influencing that decision. (If only things were that simple!) If we want to attract and keep the best, we must start paying serious attention to the many wants and needs—both monetary and nonmonetary—of our better workers.

Just about every employer wants to know what can be done to prevent the departure of top-notch employees—what it takes to keep good people from simply abandoning seemingly desirable jobs with good futures. Perhaps only one company in twenty, however, conducts exit interviews.

These are interviews conducted with departing employees to ensure that the cessation of relations is businesslike and professional, and to discover the differing reasons people have for leaving what we see to be a good job. Whether or not you conduct such interviews, however (and you should), there is another reliable source for defining the common dissatisfactions of desirable employees, namely the international brotherhood of headhunters. After all, it is they who must define and capitalize on the better-than-average worker's dissatisfactions and desires in the first place.

CLAMPERS

Headhunters use the mnemonic *CLAMPERS* to define key areas of dissatisfaction common to most workers, and to examine closely the motivations of their potential candidates. *CLAMPERS* stands for challenge, location, advancement, money, prestige and pride, equal treatment for equal competence, respect and recognition, and security.

As employers, we can do something to improve the employee's own perceived satisfaction in all eight areas. In other words, if we learn what is underneath the mnemonic, what unmet needs typically justify a person's leaving one company for another, we can go a long way toward keeping the employee from ever falling into the hands of the headhunter!

■   *C is for Challenge and Communication*

The last quarter century or so has been marked in the United States by the maturation of the best educated and most affluent society the world has ever known. The turbulent events of the '60s and '70s (which were, in turn, traceable to the remarkable economic expansion that took place immediately after World War II) altered forever the way people related to their jobs and the world around them. Depression-era attitudes—that men ought to comprise the bulk of the work force, that a worker was expected to get one job and stick to it thankfully for life, that an "erratic" work history marked one for failure—no longer held sway. Americans developed a healthy interest in having a greater say over the important events of their lives, and that emphatically included the workplace. The trend has increased steadily, and the new work force of the '90s is vocal and determined to be heard.

This brings us to one of the most common reasons for employee departure: lack of challenge and/or poor communication with those assigning work. Too often, we have workers who do not feel their skills are being fully utilized and who don't feel appreciated. There is no one paying attention, no one to say, "Hey, that was a great job! What would you like to get your teeth into next?" Such employees feel (often rightly) that communication in the corporation is one-way: downwards. The result: they leave in search of fulfillment with our competitors.

■ *L is for Location*

Although employers are now beginning to show more openmindedness on issues of flex time and telecommuting (topics discussed later in this book), this remains one of the few reasons for leaving we can't always do much about. There will be the occasional desirable employee who begins to feel the daily commute is excessive, or who has just moved to a residence that's far away from the office. Acceptable commute distances will change from locale to locale. The "lost" time in question varies over equivalent distances—from the sublime and much coveted 15-minutes-and-under hop enjoyed by some workers in suburban industrial parks, to the commuter train purgatory of two hours and upwards seen in some of the major urban areas.

■ *A is for Advancement*

As the new job skills our business world requires become ever more complex, and as adaptability to new job functions and new technology is placed at more of a premium, the challenges inherent in recruiting and keeping skilled workers have increased as well.

That is all well and good—until one realizes that in many environments, the new, flatter management hierarchies give us less to hand out in the form of promotions, not more! The mid-career promotion squeezes are all around us. Even in academia, junior faculty are lined up three deep around every professorship. (And this in a field expected to lose 77,000 professorships in the first years of the decade.)

Continued corporate downsizing and structural flattening has redefined our very notion of "upward mobility." While there was once a time when regular, rapid promotion accompanied by significant salary increases was the norm, rather than the exception, this is not the world that faces us today.

What does this do to those baby boomers weaned on promotion as the major yardstick of achievement and personal fulfillment? What does this do to the new generation growing up in full knowledge that the thirty-five-year-old vice president who started in the mail room just nine years ago represents a success story they will probably be unable to duplicate? What does it do? Why, it leads people to the conclusion that advancement requires mobility, and mobility means leaving you for someone else.

And, sure enough, many employees, faced with a promotional stone wall, are going to jump ship rather than surrender their dreams. And they will keep jumping ship in the hope of finding the elusive promotional opportunities they feel they deserve. Others will allow their visions of great promotional strides to recede. In any event, a great swath of workers will have been effectively plateaued. Obviously, some redefining is in order.

A horrifyingly large percentage of companies still base promotional decisions on the occupancy system (also known as the seniority system). Those who have been around longest tend to get the promotions when they come up. This is universally and vehemently denied, but no less common for all that.

If you doubt this tendency and its disastrous implications, try this simple test. Look around your own company; consider the promotions of the last few months and years. Pick out the ones where a "lifer" was promoted as recognition for time served in the trenches. Then follow the time-line out over the following months, and what do you find? Time and again, company histories show that in this situation highly competent, valuable employees of the previous peer rank will abandon corporate mediocrity in search of a meritocracy.

This is a difficult issue, but one that must be faced squarely. We must look at how we are going to retain our best, and what we decide may well entail incurring the wrath of a few of the older war horses. While it is never easy to pass over a competent "lifer" in favor or a more promising new kid on the block, failing to do so may have far-reaching ramifications. The old ways were for the old days, and we don't live there anymore.

■ *M is for Money*

Very few people actually change jobs solely to earn more money, although money is often cited as a primary reason for a career move. This is probably because salary is a socially acceptable reason for departure, "upward mobility" being a pervasive value in our society. Yet the headhunters, whose living depends on an ability to evaluate professional motivations, will tell you that cash, in and of itself, is rarely the only major motivating factor.

This is not really so surprising when we look at motivated and proud people in any area of achievement. Most successful people everywhere enjoy money as the fruits of their efforts, but will readily agree that it is the process and the pride in competency that count most, not the financial reward.

Nevertheless, money underlies everything. Fair remuneration, which takes into account one's abilities and achievements in comparison with others in a given field, is a fundamental requirement. As a result, the money issue is often inextricably interwoven with many of the other major factors outlined in this list.

■ *P is for Prestige and Pride*

It's easy to understand why someone might prefer to work for IBM over Last Chance Electronics, yet most of us underestimate the importance of pride and prestige in keeping the best. We also underestimate our own abilities to create a sense of pride and prestige within our organizations.

As we have noted, people spend the majority of their waking hours at work, and still more time traveling to and from the workplace. We are a world largely identified by the work we do and the organizations we do it for. When we elect to work somewhere, we are saying something quite specific about who we are, what we do, and how we approach life. It is only natural that someone who feels less than enthusiastic about the messages he sends to others on these fronts is a good candidate for departure.

Not surprisingly, turnover at prestigious companies is significantly lower than elsewhere. Companies don't simply become prestigious through some mystical process, however. Individual workers have to feel pride, and share that pride with their co-workers. Managers must not only create environments where pride can flourish, but must also take pride in their people.

Many managers would be astounded to discover that their lowliest functionaries might share exactly their own visions of contribution and commitment. A company that gives pride to its people is well on the way toward being regarded by non-employees and employees alike as a prestigious place to work.

■   *E is for Equal Treatment for Equal Competence*

Most companies review their workers once a year; typically, each job classification has a maximum allowable increase attached to it. The two most common modes of evaluation each serve as textbook examples of how not to get employees to excel: either everyone within the classification receives the same raise, or the difference between the excellent and the mediocre review in terms of actual dollars is so negligible as to make no difference.

Yearly reviews (which differ from the Advancement item on this list in that a promotion is not necessarily at stake) handled in this manner are accidents waiting to happen, and are frustrating and debilitating to the above average worker. To work harder all year, to achieve better results, to toil assiduously for the common good, and at the end of the day to be lumped in with the halt and the lame is hard to stomach.

And, as we have seen, employees often choose not to stomach it. However, those brave souls who hope against hope that the company is eventually going to recognize and reward their superior efforts tend to become supremely frustrated.

That frustration is really OK—so long as it doesn't go on too long—because it shows that the worker still cares enough to get mad. But eventually the frustration can be counted on to atrophy into resignation of the spirit, which is followed, as night unto the day, by resignation of the job. Your employee's interest shifts to companies where rewards are competency-based, rather than category- or tenure-based.

■ *R is for Respect and Recognition*

We hear a lot these days about the dying work ethic, about how people don't care about their jobs or the quality of their work. This purported decline in our legendary can-do spirit is supposedly to blame for any number of ills, including the increase in foreign ownership of our firms, the decay of our urban landscapes, and the general deterioration of Western civilization.

It's not true. People are aching to make a contribution, yearning to find a company they can make a commitment to. People truly want to do a good job. But there's a catch: they expect to be recognized for it. And as if that weren't enough, they also expect professional respect and courtesy, regardless of title or political stature within the organization.

Our employees expect that the good efforts they put forward will be rewarded by the employer with the respect they deserve as human beings. They expect to be treated as valuable team members essential to any plans for success we may have.

No longer do we have the right to expect our workers to carry out commands blindly and otherwise keep their mouths shut. We've abrogated that right at least twice over the last twenty years: first during the high-inflation, low-growth, oil-crisis stagnations of 1974 and 1975, and again in the recession of 1980 through 1982. When times were tough and layoffs were rampant, we asked more of the remaining workers, and they took the bit between their teeth and pulled us out. Now they are demanding a hearing.

Today's new worker demands to be treated as an individual and not as a number; to be given appropriate recognition for contributions; and to have some input in the decisions that affect livelihoods. All this requires that we listen as we have not listened before, give credit where credit is due, and offer our employees the same respect and fairness we tell them they owe customers.

As managers, we must reevaluate our every action in the light of treating our fellow workers with the dignity and personal respect they have earned. We must increase our respect for the value of every job, because every job on the payroll is critically important to the success of our organization.

Unfortunately, though management is often good at giving kudos to other managers and to those in the important and visible professional ranks—the "heroes" and the "champions"— it is often woefully inept when it comes to saluting the troops. Respect for the individual and recognition of the contributions that a person is able to make within the confines of his job are of paramount importance in keeping the best.

■   *S is for Security*

One of the few things that has traditionally kept an employee is long-term job security. Those companies offering such security to their employees will always have an edge in the employment marketplace.

Hallmark Cards has a reputation second to none in this area, perhaps because of their company philosophy that any business downturn is a management failure and not a worker failure. In one recent downturn, there simply wasn't work to be done; Hallmark paid thousands of workers to do community service.

During the early days of Sony, management faced a severe slump. Rather than lay off any workers, the executives simply said, "There is no work for you to do in the factory, and the warehouses are full of merchandise: what we need are salespeople." The result? Overnight, they mobilized the largest sales force in Japan, and moved out the stock in the warehouses. Before long, the factories were humming again to keep up with demand.

A 180-degree reversal in job descriptions—a reversal that results in superior performance? It's not impossible by any means. There's no limit to the commitment you can get from employees when they recognize that you look at business with their concerns in mind.

PEOPLE POWER

Most of us grew up in an industrial society where, according to the prevailing wisdom, capital was considered the most important strategic resource. But the perspective has changed. Today, we live in an information society; now, because the manipulation of that information, coupled with creativity and the knowledge that comes from education, is such a crucial element to our success, we realize that *people* should be considered—and perhaps should always have been considered—our key resource.

David Kearns, Xerox's chairman and CEO, has this to say on the subject:

> We all know that plants and equipment and organization are the essential building blocks for any company. But, as my grandfather always said, you can't sit on a two legged stool. And the crucial third leg of the corporate stool is people.

His opinion is echoed by H. Gordon Smyth, senior employment vice president at Dupont:

> Productivity is output divided by people. The company that manages its people effectively will benefit from their productivity. Now and in the years ahead, that simple formula will be every company's key to success and long-term growth.

Competitiveness, that elusive ability to provide superior products at the best prices, can only be achieved with the maximum contribution and commitment of every employee. The man lauded by the Japanese as the patron saint of productivity, W. Edwards Deming, advises that you cannot inspect quality into a product; he might also have observed that you cannot decree commitment into a work force. Loyalty and commitment are simply the result of a person feeling appreciated for who they are and what they do.

To be sure, there is no accepted accounting methodology that can attach a specific value to a committed work force, or any work force, for that matter. Perhaps this tells us more about the limits of accounting, however, than about the essentials of establishing and maintaining a successful business.

As Roy Roberts, vice president of personnel administration at General Motors, puts it:

> It's true that people can't be put in a neat box in a financial statement. You can't put a dollar figure on their net worth to the company. And you can't go to the bank and borrow against them . . . (but) people—not technology or fixed assets—are what determine the success or failure of any company.

The most valuable capital is human capital; the most powerful technology is people.

Management's job is getting work done through and with others. Their success is the only measure of our success. Our future depends on our insight and foresight, on the vision we employ to master the employment challenges of the next ten years. In short, tomorrow's success depends on the sound management of the human capital entrusted to us today.

It is time to revolutionize the way we do things. It is time to tear up the old books and start afresh. It is time to rethink our corporate and management identities, to create a vision that can be shared by everyone in the company—from the boardroom to the boiler room.

Quick Summary of Key Concepts

&. We must start thinking first and foremost in terms of our prime constituency: employees.

&. Throughout the last decade, managers have sought to emphasize the worthy goals of getting close to the customer and achieving preeminent quality. Unfortunately, these objectives were often interpreted in such a way as to ignore the basic credo that *you don't get satisfied customers without first having satisfied employees.*

&. When an employee quits, it means he has just fired you.

&. These days, an employee who hears about a new opportunity will interview for it first and think later about whether it's worth leaving his job with you for.

&. We must abandon forever the "foreman" school of management techniques that emphasizes highlighting negative employee behavior, and replace it with a positive focus.

&. Home run hitters are important, but they can't carry a whole team. Developing bunting-for-a-single skills throughout the team is preferable to expecting superhuman performance from a few players.

Why do employees leave? Remember the mnemonic CLAMPERS.

- C is for Challenge and Communication

- *L* is for Location

- *A* is for Advancement

- *M* is for Money

- *P* is for Prestige and Pride

- *E* is for Equal Treatment for Equal Competence

- *R* is for Respect and Recognition

- *S* is for Security

Chapter Three

A Shared
Vision

THE MOST VALUABLE CAPITAL IS HUMAN CAPITAL; THE most powerful technology is people.

People are our only reason for coming to work in the morning. So: if they're that important, what's guiding them?

That is the question facing us now. How do we make sure that the people in our organization, whom we have identified as our most vital resource, have a blueprint to follow—a mission set out for them? And more important, how can we ensure that they will be inclined to follow it?

THE QUARRY

Two men in a quarry were both doing the same backbreaking work: hewing stone blocks from the quarry wall. A stranger came along and asked the first man what he was doing. The reply: "I'm breaking rocks out of this damned wall—what does it look like?" The stranger approached the other man with the same question. The second worker's answer: "I am building the new cathedral." One worker had a job; the other, a vision.

As managers, we would all prefer to supervise the second of the two quarrymen, the one committed to his work, the one with a clear vision of the effect his efforts have on the greater whole.

But whose job is it to impart the vision necessary to build cathedrals rather than hew rocks? Clearly it is the job of management. That second worker will not simply materialize for us; it is up to us to create him.

How many of our own workers can we say have a clear vision of their work, are truly committed? I believe we can answer that question by posing another one. How many of our people feel that the company has their best interest at heart?

A manager's success is wholly dependent upon his ability to empower others to achieve his goals.

I hope you agree that any vision-crafting we undertake that ignores what our employees expect out of their jobs is a waste of time. Not that such sleight-of-hand isn't practiced regularly—it is, and it results in what I call the "false culture," about which we'll learn more later. The salient point is, if we want to set out to define where we are going, we are well advised to listen to concerns of the people who are going to be asked to get us there. Because if they lose interest, we lose, period.

How many of our people feel that the company has their best interest at heart? The answer, according to the Center for Organizational Effectiveness, is only around 30% of all employees. That's a 70% "no" vote—a landslide by any reasonable measure. So, at best, most of us can expect something considerably less than a completely committed work force. Encouraging, isn't it?

We have ourselves created the discontents that come with working in large, modern, increasingly compartmentalized organizations. Living, breathing individuals are reduced to mere functionaries, and are too often relegated to the status normally reserved for inanimate objects. This compartmentalization, which took place in the name of efficiency and scientific management, was applied to the best educated and most prosperous society in history. This has resulted in an enigma: a highly educated, affluent work force that regularly feels underutilized, and is increasingly at odds with the goals of employers.

Creating the kind of vision, then, that will help in our efforts to undo such massive damage—the vision that will finally recapture the imaginations of our employees—must now become our overriding objective.

SHARED VISION AS DIRECTION

What is a shared vision? It could be described as the impetus, the drive, the direction without which meaningful progress in an organization is impossible.

You can't ride a bicycle standing still. Without momentum, without direction, the machine topples and you take a spill. Trying to achieve success in our corporations without a shared vision will yield much the same result.

In the end, vision is the burning desire to achieve something, the thing that drives us to attack each new day, the central purpose that provides enthusiasm and energy necessary to meet each fresh challenge. On the personal, work group, and company levels, having a vision means having clear, large goals to strive toward, goals that are shared with others and that give meaning to our long-term efforts. And by promulgating a compelling shared vision where none was before, our organization has the power to enrich itself by dramatically enriching the lives of our employees. Unfortunately, however, corporations never make changes—only people do that. And that's where managers come in.

Success-oriented management philosophy requires a vision of what the company is, what and who the company regards as its customers, where the company feels it is going, and what it hopes to achieve along the way—remembering all the while that these goals must be developed in concert with, and not imposed upon, the work force. Unless the philosophy is both understood and supported by the company's employees, it will not be worth the paper on which it is printed. It will not be a shared vision.

A shared vision, and the complementary corporate culture that exemplifies that vision, are the foundations to corporate achievement in the '90s. The result of a dynamic, effective vision can be a work force that will get out there and build cathedrals for you.

Barriers to shared vision

If a shared vision can be so beneficial to our corporations, why is it most noticeable by its absence? The reasons have been in place for so long, and are so glaringly obvious, that we have learned rather routinely to overlook them.

There are three and only three practices that consistently erect and maintain barriers to shared vision.

1. *Reaction management.* To paraphrase the Red Queen from *Alice in Wonderland,* if you don't know where you are going, you are not going to get there. There are countless companies that have no considered vision of their future and therefore can never be expected to achieve it. Their "vision" consists of waiting for a conflagration, and then heading for the fire extinguishers.

2. *Sanitary management.* At many companies, there is a clear and considered vision, perhaps even couched in the accepted terminology of the corporate mission. Yet all too often the vision enshrined in a mission statement is so sterile as to have no relevance to the people at whom it is presumably aimed, the employees. The daily management style is similarly barren of innovation or drive.

3. *Military management.* Here, management has an understanding of where it wants to go, and a mission statement has been carefully considered and crafted. But it is never mentioned outside of mahogany row: non-management ranks are still in the dark. Sure, it's nice if fifteen or twenty bigwigs have memorized the mission statement and can talk a blue streak about their own personal roles in achieving objectives. But if two hundred and fifty

employees not only cannot discuss the "vision" intelligently, but were never brought in on its development, there's a problem.

Most companies fail abysmally when it comes to telling employees, new or old, about the company game plan. There is a terrible communication gap here, and that gap—not the death of the can-do spirit—is the root cause of our current productivity crisis.

Dr. W. Edwards Deming sees this problem as extending to virtually all levels of endeavor. "A good 50% of our production problems," says Deming, "happen because the worker does not know what he is supposed to do, so he does it wrong. And who gets blamed—the manager who didn't train him correctly? No, it's the poor worker, every time." How is our vision to be adequately conveyed if even the fundamental dynamics of basic on-the-job interaction elude us?

BUILDING THE FUTURE TOGETHER

The "who we are" of a company, the what and the where it wants to be, the how of its getting there: these values must be shared and endorsed by employees throughout all levels of the organization. Any organization that wishes to achieve credibility and commitment with the new work force must recognize that vision is the glue that holds it all together. And remember, people are aching to make commitments to be part of something bigger than themselves. Given the chance and the encouragement, there isn't one worker in a thousand who wouldn't rather build cathedrals than bust rocks.

A vision is not a straitjacket. In our age of volatility, we must expect change to become the norm; at the same time, however, our companies must be "built on rock," based in a set of values and acknowledged ways of doing things that remain constant in times of flux. These values must allow change to occur—but at the same time carry forward the basic tenets and beliefs of the company that have stood the test of time.

You can't have a vision without visionaries

Finding the vision, sharing it, and making it work: these are no easy tasks. They require risk.

If we are to avoid the roadblocks of reactionary, sanitary, and military management, the vision must be understood and acceded to by all players. We who manage the new work force must see that the vision reaches out and grabs employees, makes them say "Yes—I can get behind that. Being part of this place will enable me to hold my head up in the morning. This is a team I want to be part of."

It is employees—not management—who make the ultimate difference in a company. And therefore it is to employees that the vision's message must primarily be directed. If all the top brass happen to call in sick one day, orders can still be filled, customers can still be satisfied, deadlines can still be met. If all the employees happen to call in sick one day, we are either in a complete productivity vacuum—or left watching the spectacle of the CEO trying to figure out how to operate a tape gun.

All management can do, as a general rule, is to ensure that an environment exists that will encourage employees to put out that extra percentage of superior effort. And that extra percentage is only ever given by those who share in and are driven by a motivating vision that gives meaning and dignity to their efforts. But how much resistance we must conquer, how many years of damage we must rectify, before we instill that vision!

Like it or not, most companies have an established reputation for extreme fickleness when it comes to employees. We must face up to the fact that our employees don't give a damn about the company anymore—because over the years, in countless ways, the company has shown that it doesn't give a damn about them.

People are motivated to strive for and achieve their personal goals. People are not by nature motivated to achieve a company's objectives, and they certainly aren't likely to jump up and down over employer goals when that employer has a demonstrated history of employee abuse. So the company that demonstrates its regard for its workers by demanding 70-hour weeks and depriving its people of the dignity of a personal life can never expect those troops to share any vision of sugar plum fairies.

A manager's success is wholly dependent upon his ability to empower others to achieve his goals.

And certainly, if we plan to develop goals that will resonate within our work force, goals that will be accepted by those who populate our company, we must at the very least start by taking into account the elementary human motivators shared by virtually all contemporary workers.

The new worker demands to be treated with respect and dignity, and to be recognized as a unique individual. Wise employers will build such values into their company "commandments." The employer for whom personal integrity is an integral part of all dealings with all people at all times has achieved the very foundation to which cathedral builders will flock. Such employees will relish the chance to confront both opportunity and adversity for that employer.

Unfortunately, the vast majority of corporate mission statements fall short of the mark. A mission statement is (or at least should be) far more than simply "to make money," or "to make the most money in the shortest possible time at the lowest cost, so as to give the highest return to the shareholders." While such sentiments may be laudable in part, if they stand as a company's total raison d'etre the underlying message that nothing or no one else is more important than dollar bills will come through loud and clear, to the people who matter: the employees.

The real mission statement outlines how things are going to be because of the values "we as a team" agree to share. It tells us what we are all working towards, and why we are working towards it. A cogent statement becomes the glue that binds a company together; it embodies the shared ideals that bond us together as a team.

Mission experts Laurence Hopp and Michael Kelly, in a recent article in the *Training and Development Journal*, put it this way:

> In this state, conditions are better, people are happier, goals are achieved, and life is richer and more complete . . . the vision state is where personal values are realized as daily events. An organizational vision should articulate a clear picture of the optimal state of the company, or unit.

They go on to explain that a vision (and therefore the statement of that vision) should itself motivate people to action; in other words, it should become a rallying cry that spells out the tangible and intangible benefits of association. Prominent on the list, they further advise, must be concern and recognition for the employee.

Miller Brewing, a company renowned for integrity and resulting loyalty, communicates their mission statement in something they call the Miller Management Philosophy. Miller's senior vice president of operations, Allen Schumer, declares:

> Recognizing that our most important resource is our people, we establish a two-way dialogue.
>
> We are committed to creating a climate that encourages teamwork and accelerates the personal development of each employee. That's our responsibility.
>
> We also expect something in return. While we strive to employ people of the highest quality, we also expect our employees to strive for superior performance in everything they do. Our employees are expected to learn all they can about their jobs, and are encouraged to take an active role in influencing the decisions affecting their jobs.

Such a message not only reaches through all the ranks at Miller, it extends far beyond the company doors. It has, in fact, made Miller one of the most sought-after employers in America.

Ryder, the Florida-based rental truck company, is another highly esteemed outfit. You know the company; you see their spotless, shining, undented vehicles—signs of intense employee commitment to shared goals—in virtually every city and town in the country. Ryder's Mission statement is promoted through something they call "The Ryder Management Principles."

As Ryder's Ron Dunbar explains:

> (The principles) promise each of our customers high quality service at all levels of the company, from the boardroom in Miami to the smallest branch office. These principles also tell employees not only what Ryder expects of them, but what they can and should expect from Ryder in return.

But what role does such lofty language play in the real world—in terms of the success or failure of the body corporate? Are the Ryder management principles simply so much window dressing, as some skeptics might believe? Far from it, Dunbar continues: "(These ideas) are very much at the heart of what Ryder has achieved. Most importantly, these principles dictate what Ryder hopes to achieve in the future. In a sense, they are the signposts directing our people towards future growth and success."

A company with character

Perhaps the most succinct and compelling embodiment of corporate vision is embodied in the mission statement of Emhart Corporation, led by Peter Scott. His manifesto begins: "Since this is the last company I shall ever manage, my vision for Emhart is an amalgam of all the good things I ever wanted in the character of a company." Those character traits are impressive enough to examine in detail here.

THE EMHART MISSION STATEMENT:
THE "CHARACTER" OF A COMPANY

- A company that is successful by any criteria (economic, human, etcetera).

- A company where more people come to work to make things happen than come to watch things happen.

- A company where bureaucracy is at an absolute, irreducible minimum.

- A company where managers always know there is a better way.

- A company where ideas—and entrepreneurs—are welcomed, not challenged; where opinions are sought, not stifled.

- A company where each employee goes home at night with a feeling of accomplishment, not frustration.

- A company known for leadership in its fields and in contemporary business life.

- A company whose character is synonymous with the highest levels of ethics and integrity.

- A company regarded as a good place to work.

- A company recognized for innovativeness and creativity.

- A company where the only buck that passes is the paycheck.

- A company where teamwork isn't a cliche but a way of life.

- A company that leads rather than follows; that acts rather than reacts.

- And, overall, a company well regarded by it peers, respected by its competitors, favored by its customers, appreciated by its shareholders, and supported by its employees.

Emhart enjoys an excellent reputation among both job seekers and headhunters. One reason is that the sharing of these beliefs appears to be an integral part of the firm's recruitment process—yes, you read right, recruitment. They take the time to talk in detail about all this with people they're thinking of hiring. No wonder so many are eager to join a group that embodies and lives by such beliefs. (This is one of the most effective ways employee-oriented firms develop that coveted reputation as "a good place to work.")

No one is suggesting that by virtue of that mission statement, Emhart is the greatest company in the world, or the only one that embodies such beliefs. But its statement certainly gets the essential points across to employees, potential employees, customers, and the world at large. And it does so clearly, simply, and in a most engaging fashion.

The important thing to note, though, is that such beliefs have been formalized and communicated to people other than those who committed them to paper—and that the vision creators recognize implicitly that their dreams cannot come to fruition unless those dreams are shared by the people who will be expected to make them reality.

HOW TO DREAM A VISION

How is a mission statement developed? One effective way is to create and distribute a questionnaire—perhaps prior to an off-site planning meeting—that focuses on five key criteria:

- What we do for a living

- When and why do we do it

- Who do we do it for

- Why we are in this field

- Where we want to go and what we want to achieve

It is, of course, tempting to assign only the heavy corporate hitters to such a planning team. However, considering the goal of the project, it is wiser to ensure that your "Dream Team" is an exact representation of the make-up of the company. Try to see that it features, in other words, more foot soldiers than four-star generals, and that the foot soldiers represent proportionally all the diverse subgroups in your work force.

"But that sounds so unwieldy!" A common objection, but size isn't really a problem here. Say you have a half dozen more people than you might think you need: so what? You also have a half dozen more people involved, a half dozen more people who will make the transformation from employees to missionaries through the process. In this instance, big is good.

You might decide to have team members fill out the following questionnaire beforehand (it can encourage new or long-dormant ideas), and have the responses of each team member anonymously collated and transferred to a master document. This master can be used at the meeting itself. In assembling the master sheet, remember that the point of the meeting is to air all the ideas, to let no single person dominate the discussion that will result, and to gain new insight on what defines and should define your company. Try to incorporate all but obviously frivolous comments into the summary.

(One more word of warning: be sensitive to the sad but relevant fact that many of our corporations these days have their percentage of functional illiterates. Keep things simple; consider strategic "pairing" decisions for team members who may have problems with the form.)

- What business are we in, and why are we in it?

- What business should we be in, and why?

- What is stopping us from getting into that business?

- Why do we exist?

- What is unique about us?

- How do things really work here?

- How do we make money?

- What—specifically—is making us money today that will not make us money tomorrow?

- What—specifically—is making us money today that will make us money tomorrow?

- What trends are changing our industry?

- Does technological development in our industry threaten us, or offer us new opportunities?

- Who are our customers? Are they a growing or shrinking entity, and why?

- What do our customers really want? How do we know this?

- What are our competitors doing?

- How do our products/services improve the lives of our customers?

- Will these same products still achieve these benefits one (two, five) year(s) from now?

- How has our business changed in the last 5 years?

- Where can we be by the year 2000? Where should we be by that time?

- What are our major economic concerns?

- What are our most valuable capabilities? How can we exploit them further?

- Who are we really? Who are our people? How do they feel about us?

- What do our formal and informal job tenure policies tell us about our management philosophies?

- How do the employees view our intent?

- What is the racial and ethnic mix of the company? Does this reflect the racial and ethnic mix of our marketplace? How and why might it be valuable to change the status quo?

- What are we doing to attract and retain workers to our company? What can we do better on this front?

- What about the stakeholders? What is our commitment to: employees; owners, investors; the board of directors; shareholders; suppliers; the local community; society at large?

Once there is consensus on these matters, a cohesive and cooperative vision of the company can be created.

How long does a good mission statement have to be? That's like asking how long a good piece of string has to be. There is no right answer. The best approach is to think of it as an advertisement of beliefs and intents—nothing more, nothing less. The statement will serve as the flint and tinder of your success. As such, it is rarely more than a couple of pages in length. It must avoid the pitfall of lapsing into acres of detail—this is something we want read and remembered, not filed. And our living, motivating vision is not to be confused with, say, dress policies, which can change with every new CEO that comes down the pike.

The mission statement is an invaluable document—your firm's Declaration of Independence or Constitution. Many firms, in fact, decide that, in its final form, it is too valuable to be left to the chairman of the board or the head of the legal department, and decide to go to in-house or freelanced wordsmiths to do the job. The document's goal is to start a fire in those who read it; it is not complete until it has this effect.

TRUE CULTURE, FALSE CULTURE

George Morrisey, chairman of the Morrisey Group, offers these words of caution about the statement's formulation:

> Don't include anything in your mission statement that you are not willing to back up with action. If anyone perceives any item in a mission statement as not really reflecting the way you do business, it will destroy credibility.

Sound advice. Say you spend three days with your employees locked in a room developing a mission statement that states as its central tenet the encouragement of innovation at all levels. If, on the job, you then seize the first opportunity to berate someone who "wasted time" trying out something interesting that failed, you will have done far more harm than good. Your company will have earned a reputation, not as a trailblazer and partner in employee goals, but as a reliable source of hypocrisy and doubletalk.

And to be sure, many firms do try to shape false cultures— with less than sterling results. It is foolish, for instance, to decide in an instant that "Quality is #1" and immediately expect employees to start working their tails off with a renewed commitment—when our level of commitment to them has not changed one jot.

False culture is doomed to failure; instilling a productive vision isn't a party game where you go around stamping the company name on everyone's forehead. Companies with truly productive cultures, cultures grounded in a compelling vision, recognize a clear, accepted set of values as the single most effective way of improving productivity.

Sometimes the eyes-front, can-do approach that is the hallmark of a productive vision can actually represent true culture within one part of the organization—but false culture elsewhere. The movers and shakers at large companies often retain the enthusiasm that marked the good old days—but don't notice its absence amongst lower ranks. This is the beginning of the "atrophy" period in the corporate life cycle, a critical period when it is easy to mistake clear, quantitative business objectives with a coherent and forceful vision. Often, in this setting, the company knows where it wants to go, but is somewhat less clear about who and what is going to take it there. The "who," we must never forget, is the worker, and the "what" is his commitment to our vision.

Existing culture can be shared through training, as at the famous McDonald's and Disney schools, where employees are taught not only what to do, but the "Disney Way" or the "McDonald's Way" of doing it. But culture is more than mere book learning. It is a feeling in the gut.

Miller Brewing's Allen Schumer has spoken eloquently about the need for engendering a culture that breeds commitment in the new work force. He sees those who try to inculcate a productive, compelling vision as the defining element of our true culture as the prime movers in a crusade of sorts:

> There is a revolution taking place in this country today. You won't read about it in the newspapers, nor will you hear about it on the evening news; but it is taking place just the same. And you are fighting it. You are the armed forces in this revolution to change

the culture of American business. You are the revolutionaries . . .
the people on the front lines.

CREATING BELIEVERS

The success of any company is invariably traceable to one underlying reason: that it has a vision, one that turns people into
believers who see themselves as smack in the middle of something worthwhile. In short, managers at these companies have
seen to it that a job fulfills its promise of giving meaning and dignity to life. Only believers will go forth, scale the heights, conquer the infidel for you. Only a vision will create a believer. And
only believers work miracles.

The key to productive culture is mutual trust. You get it by
giving it, pure and simple. As George Grune of Alcoa (another
"great place to work") says:

> Ultimately, our human resource systems will succeed or fail on
> our ability to forge (the) ultimate, human connections . . . . A trust-
> ing give-and-take relationship is at the bottom of all our planning.

Grune talks about managing Alcoans (he doesn't call them
workers or employees) in a way that frees them instead of in a
way that controls them. He sees an Alcoa "(where) we manage
the business so that each Alcoan has a personal stake in it, and
therefore a personal commitment to it . . . a place where there is a
foundation for emotional growth and psychological satisfaction."

Companies that provide this kind of environment unfailingly
attract the most creative, driven, loyal employees—because those
employees realize they work in an environment where there really are shared values: where the company's success can be their
success, and vice versa. What it all adds up to is simple: you earn
back the trust you give.

Visions, unlike goals, are never achieved. They are, of necessity, dynamic propositions: they can be adapted to change as cir-

cumstances change, but their core ideas are always present as motivating factors.

Communicating the message forcefully and effectively is vital to your company's success. It isn't enough to have a meeting, send out a few memos, and stick up a few posters. Our sense of "who we are and what we do" isn't a blanket we wrap people in—our ideals must be imbued to the bone in every employee, and that requires that we ourselves bring everything to focus on the treatment of the individual.

If this requires a radical remake of the way we run our organizations, so be it. The only other option is to continue training workers to avoid making mistakes with what is known (in worker, not management circles) as "management by criticism"—the path that, by definition, encourages our employee to do the least possible over bare necessity. This is not exactly a recipe for competitiveness in an increasingly challenging global economic environment.

The trick lies in establishing the rules of the game so participants do best for themselves when they serve the corporation well. Those rules see their first and most significant formulation in the workable, motivating company vision articulated and espoused at all levels. And as we will see in the next chapter, when it comes to new hires, the best way to imbue that vision is to start *before* the first day at work!

Quick Summary of Key Concepts

> 🖎 How many of our own workers can we say have a clear vision of their work and are truly committed?

> 🖎 How many of our people truly feel that the company has their best interests at heart?

> 🖎 Most companies fail abysmally when it comes to telling employees, new or old, about the company game plan.

> 🖎 Try to ensure that your "Dream Team"—those selected to develop your new or revamped mission statement—is an exact representation of the make-up of your company.

> 🖎 The goal of the mission statement is to start a fire in those who read it; it is not complete until it has this effect.

> 🖎 You earn back the trust you give.

> 🖎 Establish the rules of the game so participants do best for themselves when they serve the corporation well.

Chapter Four

੨੨

Vision
Orientation

G*REAT WORK OCCURS ONLY WHEN MANAGERS AND* *workers share each other's visions of the present and the future.*

But for the new employee, the first week or so on the job is often marked not so much by enjoyment and camaraderie as something approaching terror. If we accept that the first impression is the most important, what are we really saying to our new hires over their first days on the job?

Fresh recruits embark on a new job with high hopes, of course, but they also bring a profound and thoroughly understandable fear of the unknown. Assuming he has some successful prior work or school experience (and if he didn't, why did we hire him?), the new employee faces, in the transition we ask him to make, a truly daunting task. Here we have someone who, overnight, has gone from being a well-known, respected, and rewarded member of one group, to an utterly unknown quantity—a rookie—in another. And how, as a rule, do we greet this somewhat jittery newcomer?

"So: there's your desk; here are the policy and operations (thump) manuals. Read through these and they'll help you get used to things around here."

Although this sorry approach has been shown, time and time again, to be at best ineffective and at worst destructive, it is still the most common form of orientation in our corporations. For those of us who want to develop a work force that will deliver consistently superior results, it will no longer do.

After all, this is that all-important point at which commitment to the new group is either set on firm foundations or tossed to the sand to await the first strong wind (read: headhunter worth his salt). What do we expect the new recruit to think of our company if, that first Monday morning, we hand him a cup of coffee and lock him away with the rules and regulations? What *can* we expect once we tell him have a seat, start on page one, and call us when he reaches fifteen hundred and nine?

In order to turn fresh converts into committed employees, we ourselves must first commit to instituting orientation programs worthy of the name.

WHEN SHOULD ORIENTATION START?

At what point should our orientation program begin? Before attempting an answer, let's look inward for a moment and review some of the fears we may have felt when starting a new job.

"What if I start the job and then lose it? What if the new company isn't stable and there's a layoff—last hired, first fired? What if I'm not as good as they think I am? What if they have unrealistic expectations? What if my boss thinks my interview was a con job? What if my new colleagues won't respect me? What if I can't handle the work and everyone thinks I'm incompetent? What if they don't like me? My God—if all this happens, no one will accept me, and I probably won't be asked to join the softball team! What if I play it safe—and just don't start the job in the first place?"

We can laugh, but few will deny that such trepidations are quite real. The wheels are spinning well before the new employee reports for the first time: he is at a critical juncture, and his self-image is vulnerable to a degree we sometimes forget.

"When do we start orientation?" We cannot answer the question without first redefining our terms. Orientation is generally taken to mean the process by which we explain "the way we do things around here" to the new employee. But in the light of the current fierce competition to recruit and retain the best, as well as our own commitment to a superior work force, we must expand what we mean by "orientation." It must take on the additional meaning of getting the worker committed to the organization. And that commitment must start not on the day the new employee starts work, but *on the day he accepts the offer*.

Premotivating

It is rare nowadays that someone accepts a job offer and starts the following Monday; most applicants are already gainfully employed. The lead time is usually at least two weeks, and sometimes considerably longer. Today's managers, moreover, have noticed a new trend in this area (a healthy one, I think): more and more new hires are getting into the habit of taking an additional week or ten days to themselves to recharge their batteries for the new job.

However you look at it, there is a significant lag time between the date of acceptance and the first day on the job. Knowing this, what can we do to avoid the embarrassment and cost of no-shows? What can we do to tie in the new worker before the start date, to get him excited about showing up for that first day?

A little consideration is all it takes. We simply make a casual call to the soon-to-be team member and say, "Hey, we can't wait to get you on board—and listen, since everyone in the department is having lunch/drinks/dinner on such-and-such a date, I thought it would be neat if you could come join us. The whole gang is looking forward to meeting you."

Another winning tactic: try sending your "newby" out to dinner with a loved one to celebrate the new job. This is a gesture made by few employers, but the few swear by it for establishing a positive mindset and guaranteeing commitment before day one.

Other ideas might include a pleasant, pressure-free "just checking in" phone call, an invitation to come by the office for a more detailed look around, or even an invitation to a meeting or company function. In short, any thoughtful action that shows you are already thinking and caring about the new worker as a person will pay dividends.

Day One

Any firm foundations we can establish before the first day are to our lasting benefit because they give us an invaluable head start on commitment. Nevertheless, the rubber really hits the road on the day the new employee shows up for work. As that familiar saying goes, "You never get a second chance to make a first impression."

Let's remember that new hires represent the single most dependable source for our new missionaries, our cathedral-builders. It's conceivable that our existing work force is limping along with its fair share of stragglers and water-cooler-gazers. Our goal is to transform our workplace, and to do that, we'll need every fresh, uncontaminated mind we can get.

At my corporate seminars on the subject of employee retention, I often ask participants how long they think the orientation of a new employee should take. The answers range from half an hour, to three days, to "as long as necessary." I like the last answer best: it takes into account that good orientation, rather than simply burning up a predetermined number of manhours, has a certain goal. Good orientation actually gets the new worker up to speed, productive, and committed to the goals of both the work group / department and the organization as a whole.

Time is secondary: only the net result is of real importance. Effective orientation doesn't take an hour, a day, or a week; it takes whatever period is required to give the new worker a sense of belonging, a sense of purpose, and an understanding of the behavior and work ethic necessary to fit in and achieve with the new group.

When it comes to orientation, it's do it once and do it right—or pay the consequences. I remember discussing a career move with a middle manager recently; we addressed the many dissatisfactions he had with his current employer. He trotted off a laundry list of problems that pointed to an employer who gave only lip service to the vaunted goal of "caring about our people." As we got deeper into the conversation, it became clear that the tone of the relationship had been set on the very first day. He had, true to form, been given the policy manual to read at nine o'clock on his first morning; his supervisor promised to take him to lunch, and instructed him to "wait for me." He waited—until 5:30 that evening and then went home. "It was all downhill from there," he remembered, sighing. All the happy talk in the world can't undo a first impression like that.

And what was the impact of that slight on the company as a whole (above and beyond the employee's eventual departure)? You can bet your bottom dollar there was a distinct—and utterly avoidable—negative effect. Individual orientation, after all, really affects group productivity. A department, we must remember, is a living and breathing entity, where every component part affects every other component part. And just as the new worker is influenced by the group's particular subculture, so every individual affects that subculture in turn.

"JOINING UP"

It is a manager's job to make what Procter & Gamble calls the "joining up process" as painless, positive, and effective as possible. The consumer products giant found in recent studies that some groups felt acclimated more quickly than others. The studies showed, not surprisingly, that white males felt joined up fastest, and that black females took longest. They also indicated that the better the orientation, the faster everyone felt like part of the team, and the quicker everyone became productive and felt committed.

But it really doesn't stop with immediate supervisors. An extensive "support network" can often make all the difference. If we have in any way been involved in an employee's selection (as prime selector, secondary selector, team member, or member of the human resources department) we have a clear duty to do our part to make that hire a successful one. We have an obligation to help the newcomer feel pride in belonging to the group, because it is that pride that engenders the commitment we so want to instill.

Poor orientation costs are insupportable: long burn-in, lots of avoidable "rookie" mistakes, and even those more costly "veteran" mistakes—with accompanying low productivity.

THE WAY WE ARE

Communicating the organization's accepted standards of behavior is critical to everyone's happiness, but largely overlooked as a part of the orientation process. Even the very best companies often overlook the step of acquainting the new hire with the "little things" that form the company's approach to achieving goals. Such factors are too often perceived as having a minimal impact on actual performance.

Yet such a seemingly trivial matter as whether a person's desk is left tidy or not at the end of the day can take on immense importance. These issues are often the very irritants that can cause serious problems between worker and manager when left to fester.

Consider this case. Susan Price, vice president of human resources for the venerable Key Corporation, a multi-bank holding company, needed a top-flight personnel officer. She engaged the search firm of Albany-based Anton Wood Associates; after an extensive search, they found Lorraine Mariano, who offered an impressive track record with her work at software development and manufacturing organizations. Lorraine became Key Corporation's new personnel officer.

The new recruit came from environments where the unwritten rule was that a desk that looked like World War III had been fought within its perimeters during the last eight hours was the sign of an industrious, effective professional.

Lorraine was indeed an industrious and effective professional, and she got down to business with a vengeance, happily leaving a desk with tangible evidence of her industry at the end of the day. "I wasn't leaving just odd bits of paper on the desk, but great piles of it. You see, the thinking at the places I'd been was, 'Gee, we're doing so much, we can't possibly fit all this neatly into the drawers.'" Those who know Key Corporation usually begin to grin around this part of the story, because there, a messy desk is anathema.

So while Mariano was beavering away, intent on making a good impression, Price, the V.P., was beginning to wonder if she'd made a mistake. That is, until it occurred to her that she might have overlooked something during orientation.

"In all the hoopla of my standard orientation," Price admits, "the clean-desk standard was just one of those seemingly little things that slipped through the cracks." The problem was no sooner identified than solved. The lesson isn't that one way is better than another, but that we must realize differences in our modus operandi, and make sure all new employees are aware of "the way we do things around here," big and small.

Talking about personal matters may be fine at one corporation, but not at another. Having coffee and food at a desk or workstation may be standard at one firm, but an act of rebellion at another—or, likewise, fine in some parts of a company, (say, the data processing department of a bank), but not in others (say, by the tellers or customer service reps on the bank floor).

It is impossible to set down all the possible variables, but here are some of the common points of confusion for the new hire. Personal calls are perhaps frowned on at company A, but may be accepted at company B. Open- and closed-door management styles predominate differently from department to department and from company to company, as do definitions of what constitutes open-door. Asking for help is regarded as a weakness in some environments, and is considered to be the hallmark of a team player in others. A new worker may have only worked in environments where one waited to be given assignments—where being a self-starter was regarded as being presumptuous. No other company has exactly the same set of values as yours. Let the new employee in on what makes your firm tick.

BEYOND MEMORIZING THE POLICY MANUAL

Disney has a first-day orientation program that everyone—from the new top-level executive to the rookie costumed character dancer—must attend: it's called Traditions. During Traditions, Disney employees learn about the company's history, its culture and management style, and how the different parts of the whole relate to each other. They learn, in short, exactly how the company makes its complex business function in an apparently seamless and effortless way.

The theory behind Traditions (and similar programs at employee-oriented firms across the nation) is simply that the more time and effort you invest in planning for successful workers from the get go, the more successful workers you actually get going. The more time you spend in the planning, the less you have to spend correcting flaws in the execution.

Good orientation programs tend to ignore or downplay the policy manual, at least on the first day. They treat the manuals as what they are: a poor excuse for human interaction when it comes to making a powerful first impression. It doesn't take a brain surgeon to realize that a three-inch spine ring binder is inaccessible and intimidating.

Assigning someone to plow through a policy manual is a good way to "keep 'em busy" when you aren't prepared enough to arrange proper orientation, but it won't win hearts and minds. What's more, an in-depth examination of policies and procedures means nothing at all to a brand new employee, because there is no frame of reference. This "busy work" serves only to keep the worker isolated from other members of the organization, people who could be building positive experiences confirming the wisdom of the new person's choice to join your team.

Better that the mammoth manual be broken down into small booklets designed to be attacked one at a time; better, initially at least, to focus on a broad overview that allows you to get the worker involved in something productive. Give the new hire enough to get by on today, then build on the knowledge base as the days pass, as he gets involved with co-workers and the tasks at hand.

THE FIRST HALF HOUR

Your goal during the first half hour is twofold: set the newcomer at ease and demonstrate your pride and commitment to the company.

Give a warm welcoming handshake and offer the ritual cup of coffee or tea. This isn't a time to impress the "newby" with your importance by being busy. Organize time and events so as to give your undivided attention to the newcomer. Use the person's name, and be sure you have got it right. Find some common area for small talk: there's probably something your new employee said during the selection cycle that will fit the bill. Try to give your fledgling cathedral builder a full thirty minutes of genuine, no-pressure, eye-to-eye interaction and discussion before proceeding on to the "meat" of the orientation. In a hectic business environment this may be difficult, but taking the time to make genuine human contact is an investment that will pay off in the long run.

After your personal welcome, the orientation process starts in earnest. There are many topics newcomers need to know about. Review the following list. How many of the items does your orientation program cover?

"WE THE COMPANY"

This includes both the official and unofficial history. The official history is easy. But the unofficial history—the one that tells the story of successful individual struggles and highlights the contributions of people at all levels of the organization—is what will be remembered most and help the bonding process.

Organizational structure

It is surprising how few companies have committed to paper any kind of formalized organizational structure, up to date or otherwise, for the reference of the rank and file. Yet without one, how can we expect our people to follow systems and procedures? When an unforeseen event occurs in an unforeseeable set of operational circumstances, the result is predictable: chaos.

Functions and interrelations of departments

This covers not only how the new employee's department or work-group functions, but also how it relates to the other parts of the whole, as well as its responsibilities to those other entities.

Management philosophy vis-a-vis customers

This should go beyond the (sadly) clichéd "close to the customer" platitudes of the eighties. The philosophy should be spelled out concisely, with examples of how customers are handled appropriately, and what happens to those who don't adhere to the philosophy—again, with specific examples.

Management philosophy vis-a-vis employees

As we have seen, we cannot expect our employees to treat our customers any better or worse than they are treated by us. Do not underestimate your employees. Remember that successful companies have proven time and time again that you can ask virtually anything of your people, as long as you give as good as you get.

Company products and services

Describe products and services, past and present: how they were devised and implemented; why they were dropped; why they were added; which are most successful.

Road maps

Pass out guides to the surrounding area, as well as related materials. Discuss the availability of public transportation and/or car pools; where to park; and, if there is a company lot, the rules of the lot. Even here, misunderstandings can lead to a bad start. Take the example of a young technician from Advanced Micro Devices, where the parking lot rules are "first come, first served." He moved to a new company where the prime spots next to the front door were reserved for senior execs. A self-starter, he came to work early and unknowingly took a big shot's place. On the executive's arrival at 10 a.m., the young worker's car was summarily towed. Not the best way to get someone up and running!

You should also go over the location of lunchroom areas and bathrooms, recommended nearby restaurants, and company rules about eating at workstations. Enlighten the new recruit as to whether or not folks commonly bring lunch to work.

Finally, let the new hire in on the whereabouts of the personnel office. Personnel/human resources people have an especially important role to play during the settling-in period. After all, in many instances, the newcomer knows the HR people better than anyone else in the company at this stage.

FIRM FOUNDATIONS FOR YOU AND ME

At this point, try to do everything possible to remove stumbling blocks and potential causes for miscommunication that can damage productivity and, more fundamentally, commitment. Ask yourself if you and the new hire have a good "feel" for one another, and, if not, try to determine what might be standing in the way.

Duties and performance standards

Explain the standards of performance you expect as you explain the job's responsibilities. It would be wise to go over the dates and frequency of employee reviews (a topic covered in detail later on in this book). You will want to review progress, at minimum, four times over those first critical 90 days: at least twice in the first month, and once a month thereafter for the first quarter.

Behavior standards

This covers modes of address to fellow employees at all levels, acceptable and unacceptable behavior in interpersonal relationships with co-workers, and similar topics that will require review in light of your unique work setting.

Many enlightened companies, such as an Avon, are using this stage of the orientation process to engage in diversity awareness. This involves creating a sensitivity to the differences between the sexes and different ethnic groups that make up the modern work force. By doing this, these companies are saying, in effect, "We're all different. Let's recognize that, cherish our diversity, and capitalize on it in such a way as to give us the greatest possible success in our market."

Dress Codes

Every company has its rules (written and unwritten) for dress and general appearance. Whether we are a Brooks Brothers outfit or more of a Levis and sneakers operation, whether beards and moustaches are accepted with glee or frowned upon, we should review accepted standards as part of orientation, and avoid unnecessary confrontations later.

Smoking

Increasingly, federal and state laws are upholding nonsmokers' rights in the workplace and creating smoke free environments. Be sure to bring your new recruit up to speed on the relevant standards at your firm.

Time and overtime

Discuss breaks and lunches, as well as expected start and finish times. Is there a formal "flextime" program? Who can authorize overtime, and under what circumstances? What is your company's exact procedure for registering, working, and claiming overtime? What about compensation time for travel or extra hours that aren't covered by direct remuneration?

This is as good a place as any to review the often difficult topic of what happens when your employee does burn the midnight oil for you. For many white-collar workers, of course, there is no such thing as paid overtime or comp time. The traditional justification: "You're a professional; it comes with the territory." However, a reevaluation of this attitude is now perhaps warranted, both on a health-care cost basis and (more importantly for our purposes) from an employee commitment standpoint.

What of the workers who consistently get home at midnight on Friday and leave home on Sunday afternoon to get to Monday morning appointments? Who know the redeye schedule backwards and forwards? Who, in short, make a habit of exhausting themselves for the company? These people deserve some form of compensation time. If they are denied it, one of two things will happen. Either they will burn out physically (troubling enough even without the attendant productivity lapses and increases in health-care costs) or they will leave for a more humanitarian environment.

Whatever decisions you make on this score, it is important for policy makers to make sure department managers are all adhering to the same policy. For example, a field service rep working for a company that has to remain nameless was told nothing about cash or time compensation when he started a job that involved traveling two weeks out of every month. After six months, he realized his health and his personal relationships were falling apart. When he tried to talk the problem over with his boss, he was told that he should count himself fortunate to travel the country at the company's expense (a big joke to anyone who has ever traveled on company business), and that the extra hours "went with the territory." The service rep had no recourse; he resigned. It was only during the exit interview that the top brass discovered how the department manager (in a misguided bid to boost productivity) had gone against company policy in denying compensation time to traveling staff.

OFFICE PROCEDURES

This encompasses the "little things" that aren't little at all from the employee's point of view: how vacation days are requested/assigned, and what lead time is required, for instance. If such issues are handled properly now, everything will be clear-cut and above board. Hold off until there is a problem, and you'll find a wellspring of bad blood and an unending source of conflict and misunderstanding.

Still in the area of office procedures, there probably isn't a manager living who hasn't marveled at the number of times a person's great-grandmother can slip in and out of comas early on Monday mornings. Offer clear summaries of what constitutes allowable sick/personal leave, who must be notified in the event of illness or family emergency, and at what point sick leave with pay runs out. You'll be in a better position to enforce the rules later on if there is a misunderstanding.

SUPPORT AND ASSISTANCE FROM MANAGEMENT

I was impressed with what was developed on this point by a group of sales managers I met recently; they had developed a remarkable "partnership speech," to be directed toward the new salesperson. It is reproduced in part below.

> My door is always open, and you can come to me at any time with any problem. My job is, quite simply, to help you be successful; I may not always have the answer you need, but on those occasions I don't, I'll move heaven and earth to get you what you need.
>
> The only thing I ask is that you remain aware of your role as a salesperson, and the importance of talking to clients and potential clients during the prime hours of 9:00 to 11:30 and 1:30 to 4:00. If you come to me with a problem during those times, I will expect you to have asked yourself if this problem is of such an urgent nature that it cannot wait until we get out of our prime productive hours.

This is very impressive: it paints a "big picture," gives specific examples to illustrate points, and keeps things forward-looking and on an even keel.

A manager who communicates such a message not only makes himself available to the employee and shows his commitment to that person's success; he also offers a valuable lesson in time management, and makes positive statements about acceptable behavior and levels of performance in his department.

SUPPORT AND ASSISTANCE
FROM PEERS AND SUPPORT STAFF

While the importance of teamwork is a matter of concern to most modern managers, the issue is often glossed over or treated as just another catch-phrase during orientation. In fact, "We believe in teamwork" is giving "Stay close to the customer" a good run for its money in the race for empty platitude of the era.

How do you expect team members to interact with each other? This is too important a matter to be left to happenstance. Likewise, the new employee's interaction with the support staff, who in this information age play such an important role in everyone's success, is of great importance. High-handed or otherwise inappropriate behavior to "lowly support staff" is un-conscionable. Leaving aside for the moment concerns of common courtesy, we should never forget, as we review what it takes to keep the best, that the best aren't just the big shots. The best come at all levels of responsibility, regardless of title and rank. Professionalism and respect toward fellow employees, no matter what their perceived status and role in the organization, is less a magnanimous concession than an enlightened piece of corporate self-interest. Those who don't view the issue in this way need to be reacquainted with the fundamentals of team play.

Another item of interest in this area: mentor assignments. It is often a prudent decision to appoint a mentor to the newcomer for the first month or two, someone whose role it is to help the new recruit settle in. The mentor also serves the important role of information source: the newcomer can feel comfortable posing the myriad trivial questions whose answers help a new employee feel "joined up" as quickly as possible. It becomes the mentor's role to get the newcomer actively involved with the job, the organization, and the people.

The institution of mentor programs can provide you with a useful motivational tool, as well. Selection is a sign of recognition for the chosen mentors: they are identified as doing a good job, and are being rewarded by a pleasantly "different" assignment.

Mentorship can be an end in and of itself; it can also be a small step in the personal development of someone you are grooming for greater things. Of course, just because someone is doing a good job doesn't guarantee he will make a good mentor, any more than being a top salesperson automatically guarantees someone success as a sales manager.

While you will naturally try to match the mentor's personality with that of the new employee, you should also be sensitive to the needs of minority employees. Finding them mentors they will relate to will speed the "joining up" process and will enhance team happiness and productivity.

Remember . . .

Effective orientation has no set time period, although the impressions made on that first day are the ones that will linger longest. Those who take time with the newcomer on Day One can have a dramatic positive effect on performance, but the curve of influence dips precipitously if this early period is not capitalized upon. If top management is amenable to including itself in this process, so much the better: the big-shot who drops by to say hello to the newcomer as he's setting up his desk will likely be remembered for a lifetime.

Quick Summary of Key Concepts

> ❧ The first days on the job shape the newcomer's long-term attitudes toward your company more than virtually any other period.

> ❧ The traditional low priority accorded the orientation process is no longer acceptable.

> ❧ Consider "premotivation" initiatives that take place after the person is hired, but before his first day; these build enthusiasm and company loyalty.

> ❧ Orientation should last for whatever time period is necessary to acclimate the new employee to the workplace.

> ❧ Women and minority employees typically take longer to feel "joined up" than white males, and thus may justify special efforts during orientation.

> ❧ Assigned mentors can be extremely effective in acclimating new employees.

> ❧ Seemingly minor issues related to "the way we do things here" are often the very irritants that can cause serious problems between worker and manager over time when ignored during orientation. If a messy desk is seen as unprofessional at your company, for instance, find a discreet way to say so.

> ❧ Good orientation programs tend to ignore or downplay the policy manual, at least on the first day.

Chapter Five

Motivating
the Best

MOTIVATION, THAT "CAN DO" SPIRIT, IS EASIEST TO SPOT by its absence. And it is noticeably absent in the majority of our work places.

The cause? It is difficult not to conclude that many employees simply resent the trenchant hypocrisy of employers who mouth one set of standards to the employees but live by another; who preach loyalty to the work force, but fire and lay off at the earliest opportunity; who say "quality comes first," but set unrealistic deadlines and provide neither the tools nor the training to achieve the desired quality; who declare, "We are a sales- driven, results-oriented outfit," but reward those with tenure and those putting in the longest hours, regardless of what is achieved during those hours; who cry that effort and achievement and dedication always get their just rewards, yet pay those threatening to leave and those just hired the highest wages; who ask for teamwork, yet promote policies of favoritism and elitism; who cry for creativity and pledge allegiance to innovation, yet frown on new approaches, reward "going by the book," and instantly penalize any failure.

This is the situation workers are faced with in the vast majority of our corporations. But somehow, some companies manage to make it happen. Some organizations, some managers, some people seem to know how to instill whatever it is that puts that look of determination into the eyes of workers. And, more often than not, those are the very organizations we find towering over their competition.

Although motivation is an intensely personal thing, one motivated worker is a rare sight: a motivated employee sets another alight, who sets another alight, until there is a veritable beacon of productivity and teamwork visible from miles away.

Motivation, in the end, seems to depend on the individual attitudes of each of the team members. They need to feel some sense of self-determination, that they have a modicum of control over their professional lives and destinies. Motivated workers tend to have a handle on the perceived value of the work they are each doing, as it relates to their organization and as it relates to the world we all live in.

I once visited a small tool and die shop in England's Black Country that was one of the most motivated operations I have ever seen. Interestingly, of all the products these skilled workers made, not one was recognizable to the average person in the street. Neither was the environment particularly prepossessing. Well, there's not much you can do with a machine shop, is there?

Or is there? The walls were covered with pictures of movie stars, rock singers, politicians, and the like. Each of the photographs was signed, each featured the celebrity standing next to a car, and each of those cars was a Rolls Royce. And this machine shop made a seemingly insignificant little gizmo that had gone into every one of those cars. Those tool and die makers and press operators weren't making jigs and fixtures! They were building Rolls Royces fit for movie stars and royalty; they were building cathedrals. Some smart manager (no one can remember who) connected the dots and used the finished Wall of Fame as a small part of an overall motivational program. In so doing, that manager helped generate a sense of purpose in a group of workers from a field not exactly famous for individual initiative and commitment.

People are motivated when their performance and subsequent recognition of it by you and others makes them feel good about themselves. If you and the work being done can generate this enhanced sense of self, the effort you make will be transferred back to you by the worker in the coin of loyalty and commitment.

Stand on the soapbox, clear your throat for attention, and mumble something about how you need to up the jig and fixture output this month by fifteen percent. Watch what happens. Nothing.

Pull out your Polaroid, finagle a shot of Michael Caine standing next to the Rolls Royce your people helped build, hang the photo up on the wall, and stand back. A tornado is going to be coming through town.

Things won't get accomplished above and beyond our expectations if we perpetuate what people do not like about their jobs: doubletalk, worker/management polarization, and a continual crisis atmosphere that demands "extra effort" all year long.

Great work occurs only when managers and workers share each other's visions of the present and future.

THE PLAQUE ON THE WALL, THE PLUG AT THE MEETING

Anyone who deals with productive professionals a great deal, as I do, will eventually notice an interesting trend in interior decoration. Their work areas are often bedecked with one or more plaques or framed citations: from this employer, a past one, a professional association . . . the issuer doesn't matter. What's important is their presence.

Yes, the framed accolades do have an advertising purpose of sorts, telling others who wander in how good the office's occupant is. Yet, and more important for most, these items also remind the receiver that others think the world of him and expect great things of him. Top notch people, you see (the ones we're trying to keep and retain), will try anything and everything to motivate themselves. As managers we just have to give them all the help and opportunity we can.

So—how difficult is it to find a reason to give someone a plaque? Not difficult at all; all that's required is that we take the time to notice some legitimately notable aspect of performance. Lousy ideas for accolades would include consistently keeping one's lunch hour within prescribed limits or finally ceasing some long-term behavior problem. Better subjects for immortalization: picking up a sought-after client from the competition, or completing a key report in record time.

How expensive is it to do this? Well, up until recently it was about $35, but that's all past history. There are now $50 computer programs out there that will happily generate professional looking citations till the cows come home. Buy one.

We all like tangible evidence that we are doing a good job and that others recognize it. That's why another simple (and even cheaper) technique will inspire employees to work wonders, too: mentioning significant accomplishments during group meetings.

Amy is a manager at a public television station on the west coast, and Amy once had a big problem named Michael. Michael always came in late. Michael made a point of letting the world know that he knew more than anyone else. Michael never did the paperwork required of him correctly. Michael seemed to spend most of his time renovating minor problems into major ones. Michael, to put it bluntly, seemed to be the classic example of a walking productivity vacuum.

Amy did not waste time, as Michael's past supervisors had, engaging in pitched battles with him. Instead, she worked closely with him on projects (as much as her schedule allowed, at any rate), and she waited patiently for something good to happen.

Eventually, it did: Michael had a productive series of exchanges with a major donor who was angry about a program the station had aired. Instead of cancelling her support as threatened, the donor, appreciative of the personalized letters Michael had sent along at Amy's urging, actually increased her gift.

Amy made sure the story got appropriate recognition at the weekly department meeting, and Michael began his turnaround.

It was not instantaneous, but it was noticeable. Slowly but surely, over the next weeks and months, he came to realize that Amy and the others in the department recognized and appreciated such successes. And he started spending more of his time trying to supply fresh material for those weekly meetings.

This type of public recognition is one of the most effective secret weapons in the manager's arsenal. Work with a "problem employee," get him to deliver a legitimate achievement (even a comparatively small one), then trumpet it to the heavens. You'll likely turn your straggler into a devoted, industrious ally. Just as secrets are no good unless there's someone to share them, so it is with praise: make it public.

TELL THEM YOU'RE GLAD THEY'RE THERE

This approach even works if the message you're sending is simply that you enjoy being around the person. Take the group of executives at a company in Manhattan who are all sailors. At least once every year, someone has the misfortune to run aground (that's "hit submerged earth with one's boat" in landlubber). Well, the CEO of this outfit, who is not only a sailor but a Macintosh afficionado as well, put his computer program to work a few years back and started a company tradition. Now, every time there's a weekend mishap, there's also a small ceremony commemorating the navigator's dubious achievement, the highlight of which is the presentation of a framed citation—always displayed proudly in the office of the recipient.

Perhaps that sounds like a frivolous exercise to you. I heard this story from a headhunter who had just lost a deal; the executive he was placing for a 35% increase (plus options) turned down the opportunity, citing the quality of life with his present employer, and illustrating that quality with the story of his recent maritime misadventures near Execution Rock and the subsequent award luncheon at work.

"Nothing is worth more," the executive reportedly said, "than feeling that you belong, that you matter, that people care about you as a person. Damn it, I'm my company's Long Island Sound High Jump Champion of the Year. How can I leave?" Was he joking? Maybe. But he's still there.

SHARING PRAISE AND SHARING OURSELVES

When was the last time we took our staff to lunch as a group, and made it a social occasion rather than a business lunch? When was the last time we took a staff member out to lunch alone? If we don't have a regular schedule for both these activities, we are missing golden opportunities to share praise and instill the positive values we say we want to see in our team.

In fact, sharing praise is only a part of it; it is just as important for us as managers to share ourselves with the troops. Sharing is lunch; sharing is plaques; sharing is praise; sharing is taking the time to write a congratulatory note to a deserving individual, or better still copy him on a note about his achievements sent to a superior. (It's worth noting here that, like public praise at company meetings, "please and thank you" letters are valuable coins it's hard to overspend.)

A manager I know uses a neat motivational technique that simultaneously makes his people feel that they are personally uppermost in his mind, encourages them, and gives them the tools to be better at their jobs. If he reads a good business book, it doesn't go back on the shelf; it goes to one of his team members with a handwritten note about how he enjoyed the book and thought the recipient might also like to take a look. How can such an act not make a positive lasting impression?

By the same token, people who are asked for help and advice are more likely to put their all into their tasks than those given the cut and dried orders typical of the Mushroom Manager. (He's the archetypal figure, you may remember, who earned a place in popular business lore by keeping his people in the dark and feeding them something other than Miracle Grow.)

Asking advice or requesting help demonstrates both respect for and trust in the individual. "I need some advice, can you spare me a moment?" "I can't do this, but I know you can . . . . " "I need someone to give this project some expert guidance, and I thought of you . . . . " "Why is it that when an insoluble problem raises its ugly head, I always smile and think of you . . . ?"

It is said that the best are rarely motivated solely by money, that they are motivated primarily by getting the job done right, by the buzz of achievement, of contribution, of making a difference It follows, then, that motivating the best is really only a result of proving people worthwhile to themselves in as many different ways, at as many different times as humanly possible.

THE "LITTLE" THINGS THAT AREN'T SO LITTLE

Unfortunately, while much current management theory (and practice, for that matter) still recognizes the need for motivation on a general or organization wide basis, the individual aspect is rarely addressed. This is perhaps because an individual, unlike a group, presents a unique maze of details that affect his outlook, his predispositions, and his general attitude toward work. It is easy to ignore the individual. But it is much too costly.

There are purely personal things that you can do for a valued employee that can pay you back ten fold. Consider, for instance, the time a valued worker and her husband were expecting their first child. Out of the blue the company president appeared in the woman's office, sat down and said, "Well, you're about to enter the real world and learn what it's like to put in a fifty-five-hour week without any sleep."

They both laughed, and then the boss continued: "So, I was thinking you might like to get out a little bit. How would you like to check into the Carlyle [one of Manhattan's finest hotels] for the weekend? Actually, I'm not asking: take it as an order. Your suite is waiting for you on Friday night." No strings attached, no tie-in with work; just a wonderful gesture from a company that didn't have all the money in the world at the time.

The couple had a great weekend; throughout it, of course, they thanked their lucky stars that they had the privilege to work for such a man and such a company.

Then, of course, there's the story of a small company's top accountant, told to take off early on Friday and get in a round of his favorite pastime: golf. Nothing special there, really. Many managers realize there's nothing like a few extra hours off as a refresher and motivator after concerted efforts on the job. In this instance, though, the time off was all the sweeter. On opening the trunk to grab his golf clubs in the course parking lot, the accountant found a brand new set waiting.

Employees will scale mountains for employers who demonstrate such care and understanding. Perhaps the best demonstration of this is the case of the foreign-born employee who had recently landed a job as customer representative for a leading Silicon Valley modem company. He was prepared to burn the midnight oil to make a contribution and get ahead, something he did with both diligence and good humor. In that first year and a half, he received a small promotion from customer service rep to assistant customer service supervisor. Clearly we are talking about a junior corporate warrior here, not a high muckety muck.

Sadly, the employee learned that his mother was about to die of cancer. His company, like many companies, had a benefits policy allowing up to three days for bereavement of immediate family members. Naturally, he wanted to spend whatever time he could with his mother, and so flew back to his native country. Some weeks later (after his first visit home in six years) his mother passed on and he returned to work.

"Money is always tight when you change careers and continents," the employee now recalls, "and flying halfway around the world doesn't come cheap these days. So when I went in to settle up with my boss about how much time I'd missed, I knew I was going to have problems paying the bills for the next couple of months. I couldn't believe it when my boss said just to forget about it. He said, 'Look: since you've been here, you've put in much more extra work and effort than you just missed. Your next paycheck will be the same as always.' "

Recognition of a person's worth should not be restricted to formal promotions and raises for major achievements, but all types of visible encouragement for all the small steps that are made along the way. Keep in mind two key points: first, that individual recognition works best if it is somewhat unpredictable in nature; and second, that small rewards can be just as effective as large ones. Whatever form it takes, recognition ties the receiver ever closer to you and the company.

Remember, too, that seemingly minor omissions can have far-reaching effects; take, for instance, not getting a person's name right. We all do it accidentally at one time or another, but in an employer/employee relationship, this slip shows an underlying lack of caring and respect. You should avoid at all costs fumbling some name that's been pronounced for you repeatedly, abbreviating a name without approval, or messing around in any other way with someone's most personal possession.

Consider the junk mail that comes across your desk with your name misspelled. What do you do with it? Throw it out! Even if you are magnanimous enough not to, the pitch you are about to receive from the missive is severely undercut. You have already come to the completely understandable conclusion that since they can't even get your name right, the rest of the message is likely to be just as off-base.

CULTURAL DIVERSITY

As fewer and fewer minority group members deem it necessary to Anglicize their names, such issues as name pronunciation are sure to increase rather than diminish in importance. Recognizing this, the wise manager will not only get the names right, but also make a commitment to cherish the cultural diversity employees offer. That means getting to know something about the religious and cultural heritage of each worker.

Doing so may entail broadening our horizons a little, and that is all to the good. In the end we will appreciate the importance attached to Yom Kippur by Jewish people, Columbus Day by an Italian, and Martin Luther King's birthday by an African-American. (The almost mystical significance of the Queen's birthday to an Englishman is probably worth taking into account, as well.) Attention to these and other purportedly "little" cultural details will show a sensitivity that must become the rule rather than the exception.

There are, of course, other ways to recognize the cultural validity of ethnic "milestone" days than by giving people the day off. For example, the Mexican celebration of Cinco de Mayo can serve as a wonderful excuse for an impromptu party, or lunch for everyone at a Mexican restaurant. (The workers who play together stay together!) Remember that cultural sensitivity needs to be more than skin deep: Mexicans are not Puerto Ricans or Cubans. Many groups that share a common language with other groups protect their separate cultural heritage all the more fiercely.

Just as we recognize and integrate cultural diversity in these everyday ways, we must also recognize and act on the effects of cultural deprivations. Managers of the '90s must recognize that many of their best workers will not be in possession of the "inside track" oral business traditions passed down from middle-class Caucasian father to middle-class Caucasian son.

The new work force will prominently feature not only minorities, the foreign born, and the adult children of the foreign born, but also many adult children of single parent households. (Bear in mind that current projections indicate the majority of workers entering the twenty-first century will have spent at least part of their upbringing in a single parent household.) Members of all these groups almost invariably have one thing in common: no one ever told them or showed them by example how to get ahead in the American corporation.

Similarly, while Title VII and similar anti-discrimination laws enacted over the last quarter of a century have done much to make employee selection less a matter of hiring in one's own image and more a matter of true skill, suitability, and potential, the same cannot be said to apply to professional and promotional opportunities.

There is a noted tendency among managers toward discrimination in two important areas: promotional opportunity and professional challenge.

PROMOTIONAL OPPORTUNITY

It has been widely noted that while minority workers now make up an increasingly valuable sector of the work force, they are not getting an equal shake when it comes to promotional opportunities. If we wish to retain the valuable employees who fall into this category, we must show ourselves to be caring employers in two specific ways.

Firstly, we must provide the skills and behavioral training the new workers need to achieve their goals. Such training can stretch from simple skills training through English as a second language and "moving up" programs about integration into the mainstream in both social and business settings. Other topics could include assertiveness training and even, in appropriate circumstances, such delicate issues as table manners and business etiquette.

Secondly, minorities need to get a shot at promotions and enlarged responsibilities. Avon, a leader in the field of encouraging the integration and growth of the new worker, has a very simple policy: when promotions are up for grabs, every promotional slate must contain a representation of women and minorities. And if it doesn't? It gets sent back for further evaluation. Of course, there may not be a suitable woman or minority for every job, but the message is sent—and (at Avon, at least) received.

Avon has instituted another formal approach (in which they are not alone) to help women and minorities climb the corporate ladder. They have fairly sophisticated human resource-based employee skill tracking mechanisms. Consequently, when a promotional opportunity appears, those working within the arguably more objective HR function have a more visible role to play in the proper harnessing of corporate creativity and talent.

PROFESSIONAL CHALLENGE

Whereas promotional opportunity is an area that can be addressed to a certain extent by policy implementation, creating opportunities for the professional challenge of individuals is an ongoing effort, one faced by the immediate manager rather than the company hierarchy. Managerial ability in this area is critical to keeping the best of the new workers; no challenge equals no motivation equals no commitment—equals departure.

The common mistakes in this area fall at opposite ends of the spectrum. At one end is flat-out discrimination: the worker is just plain not given the deserved opportunity because of skin color, sex, age, or what have you. Fortunately, this is a steadily diminishing problem. As the older breed of manager goes out to grass and the newer, younger, more aware breed of enabler and facilitating manager takes his place, blatant prejudice is much less common than in years past.

Nevertheless, even those managers who provide professional challenge to staff in a democratic and merit-based manner are receiving unexpected criticism from the very people whose careers they are trying to further. The complaint? Overprotection. Women and minorities tell of being given different treatment when they receive responsibility for difficult assignments.

The scenario goes like this: the average Caucasian male will be given a task and allowed to pursue it, sometimes making mistakes, but ultimately, with or without help, bringing it to a successful conclusion. This apparently is not the lot of the minority worker receiving a similar challenge, who, all too often, is "spoon-fed" tough assignments and shielded from real-world risks, errors, and lessons.

It is easy to see how the manager in such a situation might suffer on the horns of an unusual dilemma. He wants the worker to succeed, which is laudable enough; but when he opts to monitor the tasks in question so closely, he effectively removes any growth opportunity for the individual concerned. Stretching one's professional wings—and in the process making a mistake or two—is a necessary prerequisite for growth.

In behaving in this overprotective manner, the manager is also (though perhaps from the best of motives) eroding the self-esteem of the employee in question. Actions speak louder than words, and in such cases the manager's actions demonstrate that he lacks confidence in the worker's ability to get the job done without causing cataclysmic screwups. Hardly motivating.

A delicate balance must be established, one that allows team members to stretch, yet still benefit from our skills and knowledge. This is most effectively achieved by combined use of a number of different knowledge sharing techniques: Socratic questioning, to help the staffer come up with the right answers and solutions; direct teaching, the sharing of our experience (both successes and failures, including what we learned from those failures); and regular tutorials, to examine what has happened in the task to date, and what can be learned from the successes and failures in the execution thus far.

Another, equally demotivating management faux pas lies in pulling minorities off projects too quickly. Women and minorities often complain that they do not feel they are allowed the same opportunities as others to learn from mistakes—because they are yanked away from even the most mildly troublesome snags.

So, apart from being cognizant of overprotectionism, we must also allow all workers under our tutelage the same opportunities to succeed and fail with new tasks. The same monitoring procedures and the same criteria for progress evaluation must apply to all under our supervision.

OPPORTUNITIES TO SHINE

In every company there is only so much money to go around, and with today's flatter companies there is an ever-diminishing pool of promotional opportunities. Accordingly, managers must always be on the lookout for other opportunities to give recognition for good performance.

These should include both tasks that provide opportunities to shine within the department, as well as projects that provide increased exposure within the company as a whole. Perhaps visiting other departments or company locations as a departmental representative is appropriate, or attending management or other task force meetings for expert opinion. In some circumstances, strong performers might even make presentations to management or other key groups within the organization.

Running parallel with this increased opportunity and exposure will be increased access to you the manager; your availability for one-on-one interaction may have to increase. Often, this process provides time to better get to know those workers who are showing themselves to be superior performers. Your personal attention—not only to the individual's professional life, but also to outside interests and needs—will allow you to strengthen the voluntary bonds of commitment.

PERSONALIZED CHALLENGES

Making the worker feel like something other than a face in the crowd can help you reap huge benefits, but you must take personal taste and preference into account here. Take something as apparently neutral as office layout. Some employees will view the physical setup of the workplace as a strict mirror of the organization's hierarchy, and will eagerly swap a comparatively spacious office for a more modest cubicle that happens to be a few feet closer to the head of the department. Other workers will place great importance on having a door to shut or a window to look out of, and will be less concerned with proximity to the heavy hitters.

Increased knowledge of the individual as a person allows you to tailor opportunities, as well, to an individual's interests and skills. As we all know (or claim to know in our good moments, at any rate), the best person for any job is the person who wants to do it. Accordingly, with an understanding of each of our staffers' unique professional desires comes additional opportunities to develop rapport between management and individual team members.

Also important is our ability to identify and offer other "non-task" incentives that will also improve productivity, including: self-improvement through seminars; books and videos; and time and support for professional association or community activities.

You might be able to allot time for workers to pursue "personal-slash-business" interests. Many managers consider such accommodations to represent a frivolous tossing away of man-hours, but—especially in innovation-driven companies—this is usually not an accurate description. IBM, for one, has formalized such approaches, building into department budgets approximately 15% for pet projects (many of which have ultimately become multi-million-dollar revenue generators over the years). Penny-pinching for its own sake can have its drawbacks.

As the management at Big Blue seems to have grasped, things only get accomplished above and beyond our expectations when people enjoy doing them.

THE BAD OLD DAYS

"You aren't here to think; you're here to work!"

Just about everyone in today's work force has heard that phrase at some time or another. We have been perhaps too slow to recover from the fallout that accompanied this once-prevalent mindset. Efficiency experts, time and motion experts, piece rates, doing it by the numbers: all these and more are the legacy (if not the brainchild) of Frederick Winslow Taylor, father of scientific management. Winslow's philosophies made up the single most influential management style of the 20th century. Its precepts are simple.

Workers, according to this school, are essentially lackadaisical drones at best, without the will or desire to make a voluntary contribution. As far as self-fulfilling prophecies go, this one is among the most dependable.

Although they are fast becoming the minority, the scientific manager and his progeny, alas, still clutter up too many offices in our companies—sometimes very high offices indeed.

It is not difficult to understand how and why Wilson's philosophies caught on: they were simple, and there was a time in our economic development when they did comparatively little damage. But the days of black and white answers have passed. Business life is more complex than ever. Today's manager can no longer succeed as the corporate equivalent of a regimental sergeant major, nor can he swing to the other side of the pendulum, adhering to the suicidal style best summarized as "keep 'em happy at all costs, and avoid conflict like the plague."

The challenge now is to recognize that today's workers present such abundant talent, knowledge, and diversity that we stand to gain far more from a partnership with them than from any adversarial relationship. The old, simplistic management approaches, used with these workers, undercut productivity to such a degree that they render themselves—finally—useless.

We must now recognize what workers have been trying to say for years, and act on it for everyone's benefit. The task before us is no longer that of "managing workers" as though they were static and simple things, but rather to establish, nurture, and maintain productive relationships with all of our people, understanding all the while that each of the relationships is going to be in a constant state of flux.

Employee retention and motivation is only possible when you understand and satisfy your employee's productive needs and aspirations. Malcolm Macoby, a leading management theorist, puts it this way in his book *Why Work*: "The leader needed . . . (is) not the expert/father figure or the charismatic innovator, but rather one who balances higher values—integrity, expert knowledge, innovation, responsiveness, equity—with pragmatic toughness and skill in facilitation and dialogue." The new worker believes in and demands a right to continuing support, starting at orientation and proceeding and metamorphosing throughout the relationship as competence develops.

That metamorphosis—otherwise known as the career path—is dependent in large measure on how the employee sees himself in relation to his job. How much can we influence that perception in "designing" the job? Quite a bit, as we'll learn in the next chapter.

Quick Summary of Key Concepts:

- Unmistakable recognition of an employee's achievements—in the form of plaques, citations, public praise, and the like—is a powerful motivating force.

- Asking advice or requesting help demonstrates both respect for and trust in the individual.

- Supposedly "little" details—getting someone's name right, showing consideration for personal problems, offering appropriate tokens of appreciation—can have a dramatic positive effect on productivity.

- Motivating the best is really only a result of proving people worthwhile to themselves in as many different ways, at as many different times as humanly possible.

- Sensitivity to cultural diversity is essential when dealing with today's work force.

- Increased knowledge of the individual as a person allows you to tailor opportunities to an employee's interests and skills.

Chapter Six

Job
Enrichment

TODAY'S EMPLOYERS, MORE THAN EVER BEFORE, MUST be sensitive to the needs and aspirations of their workers. Flexibility in structuring jobs is an excellent place to start—as is listening to employee comments in order to develop challenging and attainable goals.

THE DOUBLE-EDGED SWORD

We noted a little earlier that contemporary managers are presented with the best-educated work force in our history. This is a sword that cuts both ways, however. We also have the work force with the highest expectations—expectations we as employers would be prudent to read as "demands."

In the early 1900s, we were awarding fewer than 30,000 bachelor's degrees a year. Over the last decade, since 1980, we have continued to accelerate the pace exponentially, and are now graduating 1,000,000. Nowadays about a third of our work force has at least some college education, certainly a major change compared to the first half of this century.

Today's employees expect more than a job and a paycheck; they expect meaningful and fulfilling work; they expect to be challenged. And in an age where we spend the majority of our waking hours at work, we are faced with a work force that expects not only fulfilling work, but also an employer who recognizes and responds to the realities of personal circumstances that undercut the very foundations of the traditional 40-hour work week.

ON-THE-JOB FULFILLMENT

The great majority of our workers—both in the factory and behind desks and computer terminals—have little knowledge of how their efforts contribute to the finished product or service. Without this very basic knowledge, they are unable to validate themselves as contributors.

Such circumstances provide us with a window of opportunity. The manager who wishes success in the '90s must begin to focus the efforts of workers not on mundane individual tasks but on long-term goals—cathedrals, if you will—by keeping employees challenged and helping them to realize their personal dreams by realizing those of the company. This is professional validation, and at its cornerstone are some familiar ideas.

A manager's success is wholly dependent upon his ability to empower others to achieve his goals; great work occurs only when managers and workers share each other's visions of the present and future.

There are two steps in the process of professional validation. The first, building the jobs, will be the subject of this chapter. The simultaneous effort to create a sympathetic "workstyle" will be discussed in the next.

JOB ENRICHMENT

The right attitude toward the new work force is perhaps best exemplified by Allen Schumer, senior vice president of operations at Miller Brewing. "It's generally assumed," says Schumer, "that when we hire someone, the new employee comes on the job with certain talents and abilities. He or she can handle certain responsibilities and can be trusted to make certain judgments. Otherwise we wouldn't hire them. Nor would you."

This underlying respect for and belief in the individual employee is what has made Miller's job enrichment programs some of the most successful in recent years (though the programs—perhaps because of their success—have taken hits during recent union contract negotiations).

Job enrichment, in its many manifestations, capitalizes on professional abilities and personal skills, and allows industrious employees to focus on something other than a narrow job description. Management respects the judgment of employees, and recognizes that, assuming the workers were hired correctly in the first place, they know a significant amount already and can be trusted to do their best to make a positive impact in many areas from day one.

Job enrichment is not a project, a one-time effort at improvement. It isn't something to be tried for a season and abandoned the next. Job enrichment is nothing less than the full employment of the worker's talents and ideas. This, after all, is what our businesses need most, and what our employees are yearning to contribute. Job enrichment is a continuing process of nurturing participation over numerous projects. It doesn't take place spontaneously; it must be initiated and maintained by management. Its end results—better products, better services, and better organizations—justify whatever initial difficulty we may have adjusting to it.

JOB ENRICHMENT TEAMS

Job enrichment teams, our "how-can-we-make-this-better-and-more-rewarding" groups, come in a variety of forms. They can be groups of "subject matter experts," employees from within a single area who focus on issues within a particular specialty. Alternatively, the teams can be made up of multi-disciplined teams of employees from various departments developing strategies for a number of projects at the same time.

Whatever their composition, strong job enrichment teams won't just happen. They need our help. Remember, most employees have never worked in an environment where they have any real say in how the work they know best is to be done. Taking people out of dreary—but comfortably familiar—routines won't be easy.

If job enrichment teams are founded on one single idea, that idea is communication. There are a number of things we can do to ensure the healthy give-and-take that serves as the cornerstone for team success: company communication meetings are a good place to start.

Typically, the communication meeting offers senior management the chance to review the "State of the Union" by letting the troops know about goals, past performance, and general business conditions. In return, management gets the facts right from the worker's mouths.

Partnership is the key idea here. Some years ago, Miller Brewing's Irwindale, California, plant formed a Union/Management Committee to serve as a panel at such meetings, answer questions from the floor, and, most important, listen to employee concerns and ideas.

This is not to suggest that all job enrichment meetings are limited to big in-person gatherings on shop floors or in meeting rooms. Many of the widely scattered companies are making use of conference calls and teleconferencing in this area. With such technology at our disposal, there is really no reason for team leaders not to share ideas, problems, and challenges on a regular basis, regardless of the distances involved.

CHALLENGES

Ultimately, of course, the goal is not so much to gather key employees together and lecture them about upcoming quotas, but to get them humming about what they themselves want to accomplish. And once that happens, you'll probably find a healthy sense of competition developing between the various teams. Many managers make an open attempt to develop such competition, and win positive results.

Inter-team challenges encourage productivity, communication, and camaraderie. While the nature of the challenge depends on the nature of the teams, the goals don't have to be all that serious to be effective. Remember, the name of the game is commitment, not trudging ahead mournfully towards this month's target.

Take the case of Canadian entrepreneur Chris Menard's Contact Human Resources Group. This is a sales-based organization whose six offices have ongoing group incentive programs, the most famous of which incorporates the dreaded Baryshnikov, a well-known chicken who frequents the Contact offices.

One August, Menard's company broke all previous team records, and Baryshnikov was the main reason. How did a chicken come to initiate a productivity surge?

Suffice to say that if you work at Contact, you don't want to see too much of the infamous bird. Each month the lowest producing office in their system receives Baryshnikov, complete with noose around the neck, by express mail. (Animal lovers can rest easy: he's one of those rubber gag varieties.) Upon receipt, Baryshnikov must be hung in the front lobby in full view for one month. Now you see why he arrives by express mail.

It all started this way. Menard was scheduled to be away from work for a whole month on an important overseas trip. In discussions with team leaders, Chris asked what could be done over that month to improve performance. A week later the proposal came back. Could the company set up some sort of incentive program? Menard's response was simple: "You can do anything you want—as long as it doesn't cost anything." In conjunction with the no-budget Baryshnikov plan that arose from this stricture, Menard agreed to perform the services of maid for one full day for every office that exceeded its previous production record.

The program was (and remains) a rousing success, and the story of Baryshnikov's genesis has won a place in the company lore. Never have so many people had so much fun working so hard to get a maid . . . and get rid of a chicken.

Or consider Ford Motor Company's Dearborn glass plant. Job enrichment team members there thought they could design and build a substantially improved forming oven and conveyor system. The job was up for grabs to outside contractors as well, but, as it turned out, the team's proposal was, in the words of those reviewing the bids, "clearly superior." The Ford employees not only won the job, they completed it a month ahead of schedule and saved the company $400,000. Said Phillip Caldwell, the Ford chairman, "I'm not sure that prior to [job enrichment programs], we would have asked their opinion on the matter."

And down in Fort Worth, Texas, at a Miller Brewing facility, another team developed a paper reclamation project which, in its first year saved $6000 in a control program, and $50,000 in its first full year as a plant-wide project.

OPEN EARS

Your job enrichment program's structure and execution are up to you. The details will vary according the environment in which your people work every day; only you can come up with and institute a program that will "stick." But there are some common elements among the successful programs: they all make a point of elucidating and acting on worker comments, criticisms, and ideas; they all empower workers to take on company goals as their own; they all allow a certain flexibility with job descriptions in order to encourage innovation and risk-taking; and they all are overseen by management that is actually willing to listen.

That last factor is perhaps the most important, the cornerstone of the whole structure. Genuine, non-judgmental listening is imperative if you are to enrich the jobs of your employees. Once you have made the commitment to listen to the problems your workers face and, just as crucial, to the potential solutions they devise, virtually nothing is impossible.

Quick Summary of Key Concepts

- ❧ Today's employees expect more than a job and a paycheck; they expect meaningful and fulfilling work, and they expect to be challenged.

- ❧ Job enrichment, in its many manifestations, capitalizes on professional abilities and personal skills, and allows industrious employees to focus on something other than a narrow job description.

- ❧ Job enrichment is not a project to be tried for one season and abandoned the next; it is the full employment of the worker's talents and ideas.

- ❧ Job enrichment teams can encourage innovation, increase productivity, and increase job satisfaction.

- ❧ Inter-team challenges can deliver impressive results.

- ❧ Genuine, non-judgmental listening is imperative if you are to enrich the jobs of your employees.

Chapter Seven

❧

Adjusting to the New Work Force

OUR AVAILABLE WORK FORCE IS CAUGHT IN A SHARP demographic tailspin. By the year 2030, deaths are projected to exceed births in the United States. To maintain our present population, we would need to maintain a 2.1 fertility rate, something we haven't achieved since the Johnson administration. In fact, our fertility rate in this country for the past twenty years has hovered around 1.8, and seems unlikely to improve. The message? Tough times are ahead for companies trying to attract and keep the best.

Our unprecedented affluence has led to the DINKY (Dual Income, No Kids Yet) phenomenon. Many in our highly developed economy are opting to have children later and later in life, and even when childrearing commences, the traditional desire for large families seems entirely absent. In less developed societies, large families spelled security for the parents in old age and were desirable. (To be sure, this is still very much the case in most of the poorer countries.) Today, however, in the more developed societies, large families seem to signify not security, but tuition, orthodontist's fees, tennis lessons, and, in general, long-term setbacks in both affluence and autonomy.

The few children modern workers are opting to have, moreover, bring with them another crisis. As we all know, women have entered the workplace in full force, and the two-career household is now the norm rather than the exception.

When the first of those 1.8 children comes along, our employee faces a problem, and that means we face a problem.

Fortunately, we are finally coming to recognize that our married employees are, increasingly, equal participants in a career-oriented life partnership. But we must translate that awareness into action. Those households pursuing two jobs with equal fury and determination are now the bedrock of the American economy, and we must accommodate each of the two breadwinners in the work force. Complicating the picture even further are the alarmingly high divorce rate and the related rise of the single-parent family (now estimated to describe 15% of our households). If we do not adjust to these factors and tailor our work force to our workers, there will be trouble.

The problems are apparent right now: talented people are in fact leaving our companies in droves when we can't offer them a desirable place to work. And the crisis is, over the next decade, going to get worse—much worse—unless we take action.

If we continue to follow the path of least resistance, avoiding innovative approaches, dragging our feet to avoid realignments of the old work patterns, we will lose out to those who have more foresight. In effect, we will take our most meaningful resources, toss them onto the trash heap, and watch as our competitors retrieve them.

More and more couples are putting off parenthood till later in life; families are producing fewer children; the divorce rate is running at one half of contemporary marriages. Our employee is not living the once-common "nuclear family" stereotype; that family has become an anachronism if not an outright myth. The corporate workstyle, then, must adapt to the needs of our primary customer, the employee.

HOW MUST WE CHANGE?

The following areas are the ones of key concern.

Maternity leave and childcare

In the past, we treated women who got pregnant as though there were no question that they would leave the work force for good. This served, for a time, as a self-fulfilling prophecy; today, though, such attitudes are woefully out of date.

As we shall see a little later in this chapter, some enlightened companies have led the way in this area, and have extended significant maternity leave to female employees, guaranteeing them their job back after a predetermined period. As for those women whose employers "respect the choice to have children," but show no flexibility on the issue of retaining one's job, the readjustment has been more difficult. Increasingly, however, these women are returning to the workplace, and are making meaningful contributions to companies that recognize their needs.

Consider the case of Joan Bok, an attorney who took a "mother's hours" job: 9 a.m. to 3 p.m., September to June. She stayed with this schedule for six years. Ten years after originally establishing this flexible schedule, Joan Bok became chairperson of the board at her company: New England Electric, one of the nation's largest utilities. Could this success story have happened at your firm? If not, isn't it time to ask yourself how many Joan Boks you may be losing to your competition?

The "old thinking" on issues of maternity leave and childcare is not necessarily based in sexism; many who have trouble adapting to the needs of the new work force have been led by the best of intentions.

Title VII—the sweeping federal anti-discrimination law— created a workplace in which all were to be considered equal. This was undeniably a long-overdue leap forward. However, we often mistakenly took this to mean that there was no difference between any two people—an absurd idea that can lead to some ridiculous exchanges. "Gee Emily, you're a woman, aren't you?" "Why, Harry! You're black! Imagine us working together all these years—and me never noticing!"

The best approach (and the approach that is, on so many fronts, at last winning over) is this: "Yes, we are equal; yes, we are different. Our very diversity is something we should all recognize and cherish." Equal, different, and proud of it: there's a philosophy that can conquer the world if we learn to act on it.

For some, the overriding goal of the past twenty years or so has been to treat women just the same as men, and it is true that, in general, this was a great boon for a whole generation of women. There is only one problem: women are not the same as men. Among the more notable differences is something called the biological clock, the ticking of which many women start to notice as they enter their early thirties. Because there is now a full generation of women in the professional work force, there is also a full generation of professional women who hear that clock ticking louder and louder.

Times have changed since these women first entered the ranks of the regular work force. Back then, everyone thought they were different; no one thought they were equal. Now women have worked their way through all levels of the corporation; we accept (or most of us do, at any rate) that they are equal. If we intend to keep the best, however, we had better open our eyes and recognize that they are different, too.

Over one third of the female MBAs of 1977 have already left the work force. For some, the goals weren't worth the sacrifices; for others, that ticking clock could no longer be denied, and a choice was made. Companies planning on a work force in 2020 should make a point of respecting the clock, and perhaps, too, of making the choices a little less stark.

Despite the recent ballyhoo over the so-called "mommy track," wherein a separate, slower career path is supposedly established for those women choosing to have children, the issue remains too complex for pigeonholing. The unavoidable (if unspoken) suggestion is that the "mommy trackers" somehow lack the commitment to give the company their all; the stunting of their career growth is hard to see as anything other than a penalty for the decision to raise a family. There are any number of women with drive, commitment, and vision who, afforded what should be standard family and corporate support networks, can achieve career success at the very highest levels—whether or not they decide to have children. To think otherwise is to take several dispiriting steps backward.

We should not kid ourselves: women will seek out companies that appreciate the importance of affordable day care, and that are aware that the lack of it is a major impediment to fully productive work. Note, too, that despite the increase in single parent families, this is not strictly a "female problem," but an important work issue to many employees of both sexes. For an increasing number of families, childcare comprises the fourth largest expense after housing, taxes, and food.

Taken together, double-income and single parents comprise about half of contemporary workers. What is this group to do when sickness or babysitting difficulties raise their ugly heads? Bring the children to work?

I used to work for an "old-style" manager. When a worker would approach him with a problem that had to do with a sick child or babysitting, he would quickly dismiss the issue: "Sounds like a personal problem to me." What message was he sending? "This is a place of work; your personal problems are no concern of mine and should not intrude into the workplace." Whether or not you subscribe to his philosophy, the time has come to accept that today's management simply cannot afford this approach. Childcare issues are no longer "just" personal problems, but vital and legitimate concerns for every employer in the nation. If we do not recognize that personal lifestyle circumstances affect the professional lives of our workers, then they will find other employers who do.

A group of companies in New York has just launched an emergency child care program. Representatives of seven companies employing over 50,000 people recognized that the many unexpected crises calling for emergency child care were making a serious dent in overall productivity. They realized that this was a problem for both employees and management, and leapt at the chance to do something positive (and, not coincidentally, to be seen as genuinely caring employers).

Now, whenever an employee's child has an unexpected tummy ache (the service isn't designed to care for serious illness or contagious diseases) or the daycare doesn't show, instead of calling in sick and taking the day to care for the child, the employee calls the emergency child care number. A trained sitter shows up promptly. The result: no lost work hours; no effectiveness lost due to worry. The child is in qualified hands.

While this is certainly a praiseworthy program for handling the unexpected, it hardly covers the long-term problems associated with being a parent to a small child.

Extended leave

A growing number of employers, concerned not only about losing top talent today but also about their ability to attract talented women in the future, are weighing in with what to many is nothing short of revolutionary thinking on the subject of extended leave. As in many areas, IBM was a frontrunner, initially allowing extended leaves of twelve and even eighteen months.

But even that is becoming passé at IBM. Under their recently announced extended leave program, an employee can take up to three years off, retaining benefits and a guarantee of a comparable job on return. There is only one requirement: that workers must be available for part-time work during two of those three years (something the majority of suddenly housebound professionals would kill for).

The sound underlying thinking—for lifetime employers such as IBM, at any rate—goes like this: "Out of an employment lifespan of thirty years or more, a couple of years' absence is just a drop in the bucket."

The programs that have been spawned around the country are many and varied; the most important offer variations on three themes whose time has come: flexible scheduling, flextime, and job sharing.

Flexible scheduling and telecommuting

For years, it has been common practice for a busy professional to elect to use the privacy of home to complete an important project. Most of us have claimed the right at one time or another, offering as justification our ability to get "so much more done without interruptions."

Now the idea is taking root as more than an occasional option. The trend is especially appealing to new parents. In this new work configuration, the individual creates a personalized work schedule that may include hours worked from home. A new mother, for example, might choose to work half or three quarters the normal hours, with a portion of this time spent telecommuting to the office from her home via fax, modem, or telephone. Pay and benefits are prorated.

Silicon Valley has always been at the forefront of both technological and employment innovations; this is the latest example. In an effort to retain and recapture older, experienced workers, Varian, the high-tech giant, has just instituted a program enabling employees in their fifties to work between 20 and 35 hours a week. The nature of the project determines what aspects are performed where; at-home work figures prominently in the scheme. The program has also been made available to retirees.

With the advent of fax machines and modems, we should note as well that we have entered the era of telecommuting, another variation on permanent flexible scheduling. In regions like New York and some areas of Southern California, where so-called "normal" commuting can take up to four hours, more and more companies are allowing selected workers the freedom of spending part of their time on a particular project to be completed from home. (With the advent of the cellular telephone, we may even find the most trusted team members giving new meaning to the phrase "on the beach.")

Flextime

Flextime is a more common, primarily on-site variation of flexible scheduling. It is a simple and logical practice that allows employees a modicum of control, not over the number of work hours, but over the scheduling of them.

The practice can work in any number of ways, although there are two common variations:

1) to start the regular shift an hour late or an hour early; or

2) to work an elongated shift within the hours of 8 a.m. and 6 p.m. (In this instance, employees might elect to work their full 40 hour week in four days.)

Both flexible scheduling and flextime began to catch on in earnest with the advent of the computer hackers in the 1970's. Creative people have traditionally been allowed a certain amount of leeway about the specific hours they work, often simply because they claimed the right for themselves, but also because they proved that such flexibility allowed them to be more productive against tight deadlines. The computer companies realized that when you asked people to give the extra effort that sometimes required 70- and 80-hour weeks, something had to give from the other side, as well.

Nowadays, with literally millions of information workers, more flexible scheduling is gaining broad acceptance. This trend is likely to spread even more rapidly in coming years.

The choice is really very simple: either accept more flexible scheduling and throw out rigid ideas based on a nine-to-five schedule that is increasingly irrelevant to the majority of workers

... or lose the best talent you have, as well as the ability to attract talent, to more adaptable companies.

Flextime and job sharing

Flextime and job sharing have actually been around for quite a while. Or at least since the advent of the modern hospital.

Your local hospital has probably never closed its doors since the day it opened. This, when you stop to think about it, is quite an achievement! That hospital has been there, ready to serve the community's emergencies, 24 hours a day, 7 days a week, with no time off for holidays, ever since it opened.

A spokesperson for Massachusetts General Hospital (whose doors have been open continually since the early part of the nineteenth century) has this advice for managers contemplating job sharing: "Look at the hours, not at the people."

It's good advice. Most managers say, "Let's see; I have a department here, and I can have ten staff members, each working forty hours a week." A hospital, on the other hand, approaches staffing differently. In a hospital the manpower specialist will say, "All right; I have four hundred hours to manage. What's the best way I can do it with the best people I can find?"

The phrase "job sharing" is used to describe the approach to management whereby there can be two people (or more if necessary, although two is most common) doing one job. In other words, you split tasks and hours any way you want in order to attract the right people. The concept is already spreading like wildfire in competitive employment areas.

"Except for management positions," observes one insider, "job sharing is suitable for most positions in any organization." And so it is throughout the spectrum of industry and commerce. The concept has been proven to cut down on absenteeism and employee turnover. It opens up a whole new field of available, qualified, and motivated workers who are aching to get back to work: the "returnees." These are the skilled men and women who left the work force for one reason or another and wish to return on something other than a full-time basis, often because of childcare commitments. Such workers offer experience, a track record, and the lifestyle expectations that have come with the advent of the two-career family. Offering job sharing is a superior way to attract those embarking on a second career after starting a family.

The two-person teams most common to job sharing provide us with both benefits and problems. The benefits: these employees usually prove themselves to be demonstrably more loyal and conscientious than the average worker. In fact, as one manager notes, "Even when one member of a job sharing team leaves, you have a built-in recruiter in the other team member: someone who is highly motivated to find not only a replacement, but a properly qualified and willing replacement."

The drawbacks: because there are two people doing one job, the manager is responsible for establishing the consistent paper trails necessary for the other team member to function effectively. This may require some skill development from one or both parties. Fortunately, leaving good paper trails is in the best interests of both team members, so this is a hurdle that is usually easily overcome. In addition, team members must be aware from the outset that they have a responsibility to be available by phone to field questions from their teammate. Again, however, this can serve as a built-in motivation to generate the proper paperwork.

Job sharing usually does represent a new way of doing things for management. While the focus does indeed move from managing ten people to, say, managing four hundred hours, there may be many more people to manage than previously. The biggest challenge is that of scheduling, which can, it must be admitted, be quite a pain until you get the hang of it. Until you become acclimated, just keep thinking of the new, motivated workers coming your way, and the low turnover rates they bring with them.

There are companies who shortsightedly look at job sharing as a great way to chisel on benefits, perhaps because they don't see job sharing as the long-term remedy it will become. Short-changing job sharers on benefits will do little to mark one's company as a good place to work, and is likely to accomplish just the opposite. The most forward-looking companies simply and fairly prorate wages and either prorate or even offer full benefits to part-time workers).

Quick Summary of Key Concepts:

- Due to the declining birth rate, a serious shortage of workers looms on the horizon.

- More and more couples are putting off parenthood till later in life; families are producing fewer children; the divorce rate is running at 50% of contemporary marriages. Today, double-income and single parents comprise about one half of contemporary workers.

- To attract and retain the best workers over the next decade, employers will have to show innovation and flexibility in a number of areas, including:

    Maternity leave and childcare

    Extended leave

    Flexible scheduling

    Permanent flexible scheduling

    Flextime

    Job sharing

Chapter Eight

Career Paths

AS WE HAVE NOTED, MORE AND MORE PEOPLE ARE chasing fewer and fewer promotional opportunities. The '90s will present us with distinct employee constituencies whose career goals we will have to satisfy somehow . . . the question is, how?

THE UPWARD CLIMB

Take a quarter-century of the burgeoning technology economy, combine it with a relatively young work force often requiring close supervision, and what do you get? Three business generations weaned and raised on the perception that success is to be judged on the rapidity with which promotions come along. The first of these generations is today near the helm. The second is being arrested in mid-climb, because there simply aren't the management layers there used to be. The third is that new generation who have just entered or are poised on the brink of the corporate world. They have all grown up with expectations of the same rapid promotion experienced by their predecessors, but for the most part they have stalled out.

These, then, are the main constituencies whose desires we will have difficulty satisfying, simply because of changes in the availability of promotional opportunities. There is also a growing fourth constituency, a splinter group, if you will, made up of refugees from the other three groups. These people don't want to follow the traditional road of promotion into management: who needs the headaches? They'd rather make their mark with individual contributions, or as part of a highly skilled and productive group of professionals. They want to be recognized, rewarded, and managed with the respect they have earned.

According to present thinking in the majority of our corporations, the more people you manage the more successful you are. Without the management appellation, regardless of one's competency or level of contribution, it is difficult for the vast majority to get anywhere near the level of compensation they might deserve. Each of the four groups is coming to recognize this.

Unfortunately, our "remuneration for rank" approach is a problem that must be laid at the door of the Human Resources department. How many managers have gone to bat for a worthwhile worker only to be told, "He can't possibly have more money; he's already at the top of his range for the title"?

The title/compensation dilemma we face today can be directly traced to the policies we live by, but which were created in another era for another system of recognition and reward. Bearing these constraints in mind, we must work to develop a promotional system that will serve to keep our employees motivated, fulfilled, and productive.

We start, not by assigning tasks, but by asking the employee where he wants to go.

CHARTING THE PATH

Ceaseless, full-time employee advocacy is a hallmark of those managers who generate intense loyalty from their subordinates. Such advocacy not only simplifies decisions when it's time to give out (and justify) raises, it also facilitates new professional challenges and promotions.

These same managers, of course, have taken the time to find out what sort of career ladder (if any) their workers anticipate traveling. Just as important as determining the employee's stated goals, though, is the process of verifying those goals. This is not meant to be condescending to the employee, but rather to take into account the "gut" objectives that sometimes don't show through what a worker says he wants.

While it is true that the vast majority of today's professional work force claim advancement as their primary goal (and often as their only reason for showing up at all), these claims warrant close scrutiny. There are those who sincerely yearn to climb the traditional corporate ladder; at the same time, however, there are those who want the climb without the effort, those who just want to be left alone, and those who, while not wanting to appear less than industrious, actually want a climb up the traditional corporate career ladder like they want a kick in the head.

Given a staff of just a half-dozen people, you would probably have representatives of each of these types. The question is, how to determine who's who, why they feel the way they do, and what actions you will subsequently take as a result of that knowledge. Ideally, you will develop personal career plans for each of your people, based on an a Socratic approach where the employee in question develops both the ultimate and intermediary career goals, and comes to appreciate the details of the steps necessary to progress from one stage to the next.

This procedure may require one or two meetings to get everything nailed down, but it is time well spent. Your aim is to have the employee tell you both where he wants to go, what it will take to get there, and what he will commit to do to achieve that goal. Remember, *great work occurs only when managers and workers share each other's visions of the present and the future.*

SOCRATIC REALITY CHECKS

Here are some key questions and concepts to help you through the process.

Where do you want to be three to five years from now?

Without a firm goal, one both you and the employee can agree on, nothing will be achieved.

It would be nice if the answer to this question were always carefully reasoned. All too often, it isn't. Take, for example, the junior accountant who replies that he'd like to be vice president of finance in three years. We know that the necessary steps between his current job and his stated goal simply can't be made in that time period. The necessary skills and experience could never be compressed into the time slot he's using. (Besides which, you didn't know you were looking for a job until this young bean counter showed up.)

The Socratic approach would be to ask the junior accountant to trace the path he has identified.

How many titles are there between here and there?

The response you hear should sound something like this: "Accountant, senior accountant, accounting supervisor, accounting manager, assistant controller, controller, vice president of finance." With each title he mentions, the employee is laying the foundations for a reevaluation of his stated goal.

Once the list is complete, you respond with another question.

Well, Paul, you've told me that there are probably six different job titles standing between you and your goal, each of which has its own specialized series of skills to master. While I applaud your wish to climb to the heights, I think you'll agree that climb might not be completed in the next three years. What we need to do is establish some stepping stones. Which job title of the ones you've mentioned would make a good short-term objective?

No matter what the employee says next, your goal now is not to agree or disagree with the answer, but rather to recognize objectivity displayed by the employee in framing the response.

I agree; that could be much more achievable within the time frame.

Then continue with your Socratic approach.

What do think a _____ does on a day to day basis?

What problems must a _____ be capable of handling?

What do you think are the most exciting parts of a _____'s job? The least exciting?

What you are doing is providing a "Socratic reality check." Listen to each answer closely; try to highlight any omissions the employee may make. Continue with:

What are the skills and personal attributes that someone in this position must possess to do the job successfully?

If the employee has difficulty in answering, help him along.

Try thinking of the best _____ you know; what made that person so special?

Now think of the worst _____ you know; what were that person's biggest faults?

The next steps come logically.

From where you stand now, what skills and other attributes have you got to develop to give you what it takes to become a _____?

What is all this going to require of you in terms of personal and professional effort and time?

From here you will go into planning the specific steps necessary to achieve the realistic career objective.

IDENTIFYING MEANINGFUL GOALS

A little earlier, I said that this process will sometimes take more than one meeting. This is because, on occasion, the employee you walk through it will be woefully unprepared. In such a case, offer one or two of the questions as informal assignments for the next meeting.

It is as a direct result of such "Socratic reality checks" that employees come to terms with realistic career goals. Often, that desire to become "the big enchilada" is in reality simply peer or familial pressure: you were receiving an "expected response" delivered by habit as a result of years of conditioning.

Taking each of your workers through these few simple steps will allow many of them to recognize that their shining career goal isn't really so important that they are prepared to start evening classes again, or put in the extra personal time to achieve the putative goal.

Commitments

Once a firm goal has been agreed upon, it's time to make commitments. What is the employee going to do to achieve the objective? What can you and the company do to support these goals? (Your response here might include formal courses, professional association activities, especially relevant assignments, temporary job rotation, in-house training, or on-the-job training.)

You must also assess how the employee's current performance puts them on track to the desired objective, and make a careful analysis of the cracks. On the manager's list of least desirable ways to spend an hour, discussing an employee's faults and weaknesses ranks a close second behind actually firing someone. Yet this is one situation in which your observations can be put forward in the context of a professional challenge, and are thus somewhat less likely to be taken personally. Certainly, the employee has a vested interest in listening objectively.

> *Paul, people get ahead not just based on what they do well, but on their ability to look at themselves objectively and see their faults and blemishes. Taking this stance with yourself, what areas do you think you might need to give some attention to in consideration of your overall career goals?*

If this continued Socratic approach fails to yield the results you want, you will need to approach the problem head-on.

> *Paul, you are without doubt one of the most creative and brightest people I have working for me. No one in the department weighs the pros and cons of an idea quicker than you do.* (Pause.) *However, if you want to become a section leader, I think you need to give some attention to your packaging. When others come up with suggestions, you've already been there and back: you can shoot holes in their ideas before they're even fully uttered. Invariably you are correct; that isn't the problem. The problem we have to solve is getting the rest of the team to look at you with respect and affection. As it is, they respect you, but are also intimidated by you.*

Then you might go on to show how Paul can improve his interpersonal skills, and conclude by referring to how this affects achievement of his personal goals.

> *So if, instead of telling people what's wrong with their ideas, you look for the good in them, praise the originator, and graft your own suggestions onto them, people will feel better about rallying around you. They'll begin to see you more as a supportive figure, Paul, someone who's able to bring out the best in others . . . and that's a very important skill for managers these days.*

Flexibility

Career development plans are never set in concrete. As a manager you probably know this already, but you must also let your people know that it is no sign of weakness if their goals change over time. This means addressing career goals formally at least once a year, as well as incorporating them into performance reviews. (The crucial topic of how and when to conduct these reviews is discussed in full later in this book.)

The importance of recognized career objectives cannot be overstated. A manager who can contribute to an employee's sense of self-worth by helping refine and polish professional goals will make a key contribution to his company. Such mutual goal-orientation is an integral part of the responsibility to provide the company with competent and committed workers.

Of course, none of this can be achieved without a clear understanding on the manager's part of how the company actually works (as opposed to how the policy manual says it does). The challenge must fall to those in human resources and training and development to see that as corporations we walk like we talk; if there is a discrepancy between theory and practice, great care must be taken not to mislead employees. Aspirations are vital both to the employee's sense of commitment and to the performance of the work group.

EMPLOYEE-DRIVEN CAREER PLANS: A COMPETITIVE ADVANTAGE

Through the employee-driven career plans we have been discussing, individuals are able to achieve their full potential with you, rather than the competition. A clear focus on mutually accepted career objectives enables employees to take direction and see specific assignments as part of an overall plan bringing them closer with every stop to where they have said they want to go.

And with Socratic reality checks, motivation becomes less of a problem: the worker takes greater and greater responsibility for their own motivation. He—not the bugaboo of faceless, ruthless management—is responsible for the hard choices and tough commitments, the decisions to give time and effort, the determination to work consistently toward a defined goal.

This reality of self-determination is not without its complications, all of which must be carefully monitored by the manager. When, somewhere along the primrose path, our junior accountant decides the struggle to V.P.-dom isn't worth it, the manager must be there for him. As the realization dawns, the employee must be reassured that this decision does not diminish him in the eyes of the company, and certainly shouldn't be used as an excuse for self-castigation. Just as important, the manager must facilitate the establishment of new goals. Bear in mind that for some, the challenge of a goal, rather than its actual attainment, is what is important.

BEYOND THE FAST TRACK

It's imperative to recognize the validity of anyone's stated career goal, whether it involves travel along the fast track or not. It doesn't take a particularly brilliant manager to realize that accountants who want to remain accountants (or those satisfied within any other job title, for that matter) are worth considerably more than their weight in gold. However, a general acceptance of the status quo doesn't mean these people can simply be forgotten about. Indeed, being an accountant is one thing, but your charge may want to become the best accountant west of the Pecos, which is a different matter entirely.

More and more workers are deciding against the management path, yet in doing so they are not denying ambition. Many of these people are, or could become, the stellar lights of your company. They have the skills; they have the dedication; often they have the vision so important to a company's competitive ability. Far from following the path of least resistance, they have usually made some very conscious decisions about their careers.

These new careerists want just as much recognition as those climbing toward top management, and they often demand even more money. They will think nothing of looking elsewhere for professional challenge if their expertise is not listened to, respected, and rewarded. They want to reach the heights as much as anyone: the only difference is that they've redefined the terms. Outfits that want to hold onto these valuable resources must develop parallel career ladders.

PARALLEL CAREER LADDERS

In creating parallel career ladders, we are essentially creating professional nonmanagement title paths that carry the same cachet and rewards as their management counterparts.

When companies provide such parallel career ladders, expertise and knowledge stays where it really belongs and can be of most value to the corporation. Furthermore, these super-accountants, super-engineers, super-designers, and so forth are perfectly positioned to be of greatest help to another aspect of the company's future: its entry-level and junior ranked professionals.

The days are long gone when a company could, as a matter of course, take its best salesperson and put him into sales management. For companies eager to achieve a dominant position or remain at the forefront of their fields, parallel career ladders are not so much a thing of the future as an urgency of the present. With every month that passes without their institution, a company loses valuable talent and momentum.

ROTATION

The smart farmer uses crop rotation to insure consistent quality and productivity. He knows that the same crop, raised year in and year out from the same soil, will eventually suffer in terms of both quality and quantity. To avoid these twin evils, the smart farmer rotates his crops. Every two or three years, crops grown on one area of the farm are transferred to another area. Good farmers know that a single crop, left in one place too long, will impoverish the soil by overloading it with some things and denuding it of others. They realize that continued overuse of one crop in one place results in soil burnout.

Similarly, one person in one field for too long can lead to a drop in quality, followed by a drop in productivity and, ultimately, burnout.

In fact, many of those you might have diagnosed as suffering from burnout would greatly benefit from job rotation and the accompanying challenge of new assignments. We can (and should) "recycle" selected employees in this way, offering those who are no longer optimally productive different assignments that offer the potential of fresh achievement and renewed meaning for their professional lives. Companies who cannot do this will see tenure diminishing, and will be unable to attract the best of the up and coming professionals.

Actually, job rotation has been a staple for some time in developing company leaders. The very techniques that have kept fast-trackers "married" to one company can be used to instill the same experience and commitment throughout the work force. After all, a team is only as strong as its weakest link!

Job rotation offers the added benefit of improving inter-departmental cohesion. When our workers understand the needs and goals of the "guys across the hall" (both because they have worked there and because they have friends there), the whole organization is at an advantage.

The concept of job rotation differs significantly from the linear track by which one progresses upward by many steps "through the ranks," from, say, clerk to departmental head. It is also distinct from the parallel ladder, where a project engineer grows to be staff engineer, then senior staff engineer, and perhaps finishes by attaining the "fellow" designation.

The goal of all three, however, is the same: to improve motivation and increase commitment. With job rotation (which can apply equally to an executive career path and the skilled and semi-skilled jobs of the shop floor), the idea is to move from the system of promoting within a specialized function to a system of promoting across functions. An executive might move from strategic planning to human resources, then to training, then to sales. A skilled worker in a machine shop would, over a period of time, achieve competence with all the jigs and presses in the shop, plus a thorough grounding in maintenance and quality control. Jobs are enriched, people are enriched, and burnout is just another word.

When our people are enriched, of course, our organizations are, as well. Job rotation means you care for the employee—he is more than a means to an end, but a valued member of the family who should not be used to exhaustion and summarily replaced.

Such attention to the employee's well-being and sense of self-worth can yield truly staggering levels of loyalty—the kind of loyalty companies these days often strive vainly to achieve by establishing intricate compensation packages. What good is a 401K plan if the issuer forgets to focus on the person receiving the check and abuses his goodwill by assigning him to the same deadening grind for years at a time? Even if the worker does stick around for the required number of years, what quality of work will have been the result? The goal is not to bribe our employees into continuing to punch a clock, but rather to inspire them to scale the heights for their sake and our own.

WINNING RAISES AND PROMOTIONS FOR YOUR PEOPLE

Most managers recommend their subordinates for raises and promotions in the regular cycle of the annual review system. To keep your best, start bucking the system right now.

Do whatever is necessary to create equity in your department; strive to get everyone on an even footing. Does this mean offer everyone the same remuneration regardless? Of course not.

However, you may have someone who was victimized under another manager, or someone who does sterling work but has been overlooked because he doesn't toot his own horn. Being known for fair treatment never did any manager any harm. Go to bat for these people.

Getting your deserving employees recognition, raises, and promotions—when these will mean something positive to the recipient—is a continuous point, flank, and rear-guard action, not an optional good deed to be carried out now and then. In addition, you must protect their rights to the tools and time necessary to get projects completed successfully, rather than offering unrealistic deadlines to keep your superiors happy. Your subordinates will be happier in the long term if they are members of a stable, competent, fairly rewarded group known for consistently delivering the goods when times are tough.

Some people need to be convinced when it comes to promotions and raises, others don't. Correctly targeting these people for your campaign will make the difference between success and failure. Does your boss have final say, or is his boss involved as well? What role do the human resources people play? How can they help you? Championing someone's cause means convincing individuals of its worthiness, of getting those individuals to see things as you do, if necessary over a period of time.

Whom do we choose to represent? Must it always be someone who deserves a raise or a promotion right now? No. Your advocacy of worthy team members must be ongoing. Look at it this way: a flame can burn brightly in your department, but unless someone caries the torch outside your door, no one else will know the good news.

Assuming, then, that the instances of gross inequity in your department have been addressed to your satisfaction, we can move on to the subtler, long-term cheerleading most successful managers engage in. The time frame we traditionally deal with is 52 weeks; that gives us at least 52 opportunities to promote our agenda. (More than once a week would perhaps be gilding the lily.) Make a point of informing key players of the successes in your area, who's responsible for them, and what they did to make things happen. Just as important, get it all down on paper and keep your own copies. This documentation is invaluable when you see an opportunity to make your case.

Quick Summary of Key Concepts

- 🕊 Ceaseless, full-time employee advocacy is a hallmark of those managers who generate intense loyalty from their subordinates.

- 🕊 The employee must sense that there is a direct link between his own success and the achievement of company goals.

- 🕊 Get feedback from employees by using Socratic reality checks.

- 🕊 You must let your people know that it is no sign of weakness if their goals change over time.

- 🕊 Employee-driven career plans build intense loyalty and thus offer a competitive advantage.

- 🕊 There are a number of interesting and challenging career options available to employees other than the traditional "fast track" toward management responsibility, including parallel career ladders and job rotation.

Chapter Nine

Turning
Losers into
Winners,
Turning
Disasters
out the Door

No ONE SETS OUT IN LIFE TO BE A FAILURE.

Most people really do want to succeed. Most people can succeed. As a modern manager, you can help your employees realize some of their dreams by helping them to be their best; in the process, you can help yourself to achieve your own goals.

WHAT DOESN'T WORK

The first step in helping people to be their best is to let them know the acceptable requirements for professional standards of performance. These standards must be both measurable and achievable.

"Everyone has got to improve" doesn't cut it; neither does "We must have a 120% increase in production by Friday of this week." Implicit in such exhortations is the belief that if we only pulled our socks up we could easily do better. The result? Good workers are offended, and the rest don't take any notice anyway.

Improving standards of performance has nothing to do with a new batch of slogans or increased quotas. Slogans are cheap. As for quotas, they are too often set without the establishment of any practical methods of achieving them—and because everyone eases off once a quota has been achieved, management routinely sets them at unrealistically high levels to compensate. In short, quotas and slogans tend to be the tools of choice for management with no real grip on the problems at hand.

WHAT IS CPR?

We can, however, achieve significant improvements in employee performance with CPR. No, this has nothing to do with hammering your employees in the chest: CPR is short for the critical performance review.

We've observed already that managers hate two things: firing employees, however much they might deserve it, and performance reviews of any kind. This chapter will address both, but the review process primarily.

There are several reasons for our antipathy toward employee reviews. We don't like to sit in judgment on others, especially when inadequate review procedures make us uncertain that our reviews are accurate. We find it unpleasant to give criticism for the same reason, and also because these meetings are usually such rare events that they can escalate into highly charged emotional exchanges, sometimes leading to open confrontation.

While we may not like the idea of conducting employee reviews, they come with the territory. And intelligently used, the review can be a manager's most valuable productivity tool.

The keys are consistency and frequency. The consistency offers the employee a reliable standard against which progress can be measured; the frequency removes much of the fear and anticipation that accompanies this process when it is conducted only once a year.

The results can be nothing short of amazing. Take the medium-sized California auto dealership where three employees were in serious trouble. One salesperson had taken the place of a top rep who had been promoted; the new fellow's results were dispiriting to say the least. A woman who was in charge of the firm's advertising couldn't, after six months on the job, seem to make much of a splash with any media buy of any kind. And her secretary was plagued by poor time management, chronic productivity problems, and a sea of paperwork she never seemed able to handle properly.

Management at the dealership instituted a program of monthly reviews for its employees; in the case of each of the three I've mentioned, the turnaround was dramatic. The salesperson, by the time he had completed twelve months of regular discussions with his supervisor, had pulled down so much in commissions that the rate of increase in his yearly income was the dealership's highest by a long shot. The media buyer oversaw not one but three wildly successful (and quite complex) campaigns within four months of beginning the new review procedures. And (perhaps just as significant in the long run), the secretary, who did improve her performance notably, decided, eight months after taking part in the reviews, that she was in the wrong job. She applied for—and won entrance to—a top business school, and referred a friend who proved more than capable at handling her old position.

That's three low-level performers transformed into two superstars and one satisfactory employee who eventually moved on. CPRs have a way of working just these sorts of changes, and they can do the trick in virtually any organization.

GIVING EMPLOYEES THE FEEDBACK THEY NEED

CPRs are not something to be restricted to substandard employees: the best team members will appreciate the feedback as much as anybody. While you may believe that these top performers are far ahead of the others, remember that the superior workers got that way because they believe in improvement. Not to involve them in the CPR process is short-sighted, and will make them feel left out, overlooked, and demotivated. Including them in the process, however, removes pressure from all other participants, and keeps the CPR from being viewed as a punitive program.

The well-prepared CPR can be a positive experience all around, as long as a few simple guidelines are adhered to.

SOME CPR GROUND RULES

Recognize good behavior and correct bad behavior, but be aware that everyone remembers criticism far longer than praise. Criticism should be constructive; you must be seen to be providing solutions rather than merely raising problems. Your observations regarding both good and bad behavior must be accompanied with concrete examples and actual occurrences.

Discuss how current performance compares with established standards. Avoid vague comparisons with some elusive ideal performance level; set specific targets and goals.

Make sure the environment is conducive to two-way communication. The CPR is not just an opportunity to get your views across; the employee must feel comfortable expressing his own feelings, opinions, hopes, and fears.

PREPARING FOR THE CPR

It is impossible to walk into a CPR cold and expect any meaningful results; some preparation is in order. Fortunately, you won't need to do too much homework. (Managers, as we all know, are pressed for time now and then.)

An effective procedure requires adherence to a simple five-step process.

Step One

Ensure that everyone who depends on you for guidance and authority knows that there are new standards of performance.

Step Two

Set these new standards to paper as they relate to each employee, even if they only differ slightly and in small respects. Reviewing these summaries is necessary to attain some degree of objectivity, a quantity too often in short supply among those conducting performance reviews.

Managers tend to suffer from two dangerous maladies when it comes to evaluating subordinates. The first is the "halo effect" that fools us into thinking that someone exceptionally good (or bad) in a particular area is equally good (or bad) in all other areas. The second is known as the "doppelganger syndrome": this is where certain aspects of a particular worker remind us overwhelmingly of another, and as a result all impressions of that individual are colored by the impressions we harbor about the person of whom he or she reminds us.

Because of these pitfalls, written summaries for each employee are appropriate.

Step Three

Along with our written standards of job performance, create a "critical incident file" in which, every day, you will note specific examples of demonstrably superior or inferior performance to be used as a basis for the next CPR.

Step Four

Set relationships and responsibilities on a new and firm footing. You must begin the review process from a point of firm agreement about individual responsibilities.

A good place to start is by having the worker develop his own job description independently, and then revising this document together until there is agreement. There really is no alternative to reaching common ground in this way; if you can't agree on what the job is, you will never agree on the execution.

Step five

Set a date and time for the CPR; at the time you schedule this, give the worker a review form to fill out. Self-reviews are usually found to be at least as critical as those we would subsequently dole out.

On the following page is a sample CPR form:

Performance Evaluation for _____

Date _____

Job description mutually agreed upon:

Performance:	Good	Average	Needs Attention
Critical dimensions			
A			
B			
C			
D			
E			
Taking direction			
Attitude toward co-workers			
Attitude toward job			
Attitude to management			
Quality of work			
Quantity output			
Overall rating			
Areas I would like to develop:			
How manager can help:			
Commit to achieve:			

It is common for CPRs to be aimed primarily at troubled and borderline employees, and thus to occur over a specific (brief) time period—say, every week for two months—with the goal of either turning the situation around or reaching a point of resignation or termination.

I endorse this approach, but I also recommend that the procedure become an integral management tool for all employees under a manager's guidance. In other words, every employee—excellent, average, or in intensive care—should go through the following process at least every 90 days. Doing so will motivate all your people, make them work more cohesively as a unit, and yield better products and/or services for your customers.

ANATOMY OF A CPR

A CPR meeting follows a simple organizational structure. It looks like this:

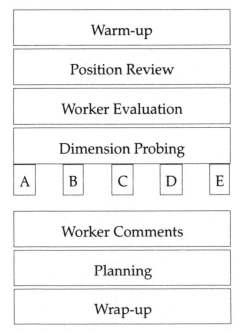

WARM-UP

You have probably noticed certain similarities between the organization of a CPR and that of a good employee selection interview (a topic covered in this book's companion volume, *Hiring the Best*).

During a job interview, you normally take the first few minutes to relax the job candidate, get his defenses down, and make it easier to elicit meaningful responses to your questions. You have a similar goal at this stage of the CPR. Formal meetings with one's boss are almost always cause for a certain modest increase in one's adrenaline level. So, for a minute or two, set the right tone with some small talk (and perhaps a nonthreatening question or two) about current positive events with which both parties are familiar.

POSITION REVIEW

This is where the two of you put the meeting on firm foundations by deciding what is going to be discussed and within what parameters. During the review, you will want to be making meaningful comparisons and conclusions, so be sure you agree on:

- The time period the two of you are going to be discussing (i.e., the past day, week, month, quarter).

- The structure of the meeting: "Paul, here's what we'll do this afternoon. First of all, we'll look at what's been happening, with you giving me your evaluation of the past week. Then we'll examine the important areas in detail, and finally we'll reach some conclusions and make our plans for the next week."

- Your mutual commitment to work together to address the problems and opportunities you identify.

WORKER EVALUATION

Once you have established to your satisfaction that, during the meeting, apples will in fact be compared with apples and not with eight-track cassette players, you will review the employee's evaluation of his own performance.

If you're smart, you will make sure that the employee fills out his own evaluation form and drops it off early enough for you to have a chance to look it over before the meeting. You should be cool, calm, and collected—as well as alone—when you first go over this material; this way you know what to expect. (You will also be in a better position to defuse those issues that could cause any unnecessary anxiety.)

The key to a successful CPR is listening carefully to the worker's evaluation of his performance against the agreed-upon standards. Nothing is more demotivating than a manager who doesn't listen. (Bear in mind the general rule of thumb that the degree to which your staff talks to you is a direct barometer of how well you listen to them.) As the employee summarizes what he has written, listen carefully without interrupting, editorializing, or otherwise making value judgments.

Listening, of course, is more than simply sitting impassively and staring at the speaker (or worse, into space). You must show that you have listened and understood: whether or not you agree with what is being said at this stage of the CPR is immaterial. Consequently, your feedback should be supportive and to the point: "So, if I understand you correctly . . . " "What you are saying is . . . "

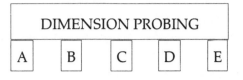

This is the heart of the CPR. One by one, examine each of the critical skill areas/dimensions (they're listed as the letters A through E on the sample form reproduced earlier) that, taken together, allow you to gauge standards of performance on the job in question.

Intelligent questioning during this stage will show that you are interested and that you care; it will also yield answers that will, themselves, direct the employee toward improved performance levels.

Following are some questioning techniques adaptable to any number of different circumstances. They are designed to keep the candidate talking, and you evaluating and guiding the conversation.

Questions to ask during the dimension probing stage

Before all else, the questions you pose at this crucial stage must be nonthreatening. Keep the worker calm. The aim of the CPR is to reach concensus, not conflict and confrontation.

Allow the employee time to think about his answer before responding, as well as time to amplify on what he eventually does say. For the manager, that means not only becoming comfortable with silence, but also knowing when to back off a topic if a worker gets traumatized. Better to come back to such issues later, once you have managed to take the tension level down a notch or two.

Framing questions

Frame your questions carefully; avoid those that will demand more of the employee's powers of deduction than he can be expected to deliver in this setting. Keep things clear. You want the worker to concentrate on answering your questions, not trying to figure out what they mean. If he must spend time trying to decipher what you are saying, your meeting will suffer.

Sequencing

Earlier in the process, you determined the critical dimensions of the position. Now you must keep the meeting in line with that orderly thinking. Examine one dimension at a time, and examine it fully before you move on to the next one.

Flagging topic changes

As you move from one area to the next, let the employee know you are changing the subject; give him a chance to fill in any gaps he sees. "I think it is time to address the next area; is there anything you think we should add here before moving on?"

Staying on track

Sometimes you will have CPR meetings in which the employee has a private agenda that doesn't match up with your own. You may find yourself listening to explanations you didn't ask for, and answers to questions you never asked. When this happens there are a few transitions you can use to keep the meeting on track:

- Deftly redirect the conversation, and take the blame for the wrong turn yourself. "You know, I don't think I made myself quite clear; what I really meant to ask you/wanted us to discuss . . . "

- Wait for a pause (everyone has to stop for breath eventually) and then say, "You know, that's interesting, and it makes me want to talk to you about . . . "

- Use reflexive questions to keep the employee on the subject. You can construct a reflexive question simply by incorporating such phrases as these at the end of a statement:

    . . . don't you?

    . . . won't you?

    . . . can't you?

    . . . didn't you?

    . . . wouldn't you?

    . . . couldn't you?

    . . . shouldn't you?

These add-ons are a virtually foolproof way to gain agreement from the other person. They are also useful for smoothly finishing one topic and moving on to another: "With time so short, I think we should move on to the next area, don't you?"

Open- and closed-ended questions

Ask open-ended questions whenever you want the employee to give an explanation. Don't expect employees to open up and give expansive answers when you ask them closed-ended questions that by their nature only ask for yes/no answers.

- "What did you feel were the high points of what you did on the Monarch project this week?" *(Open-ended.)*

- "Did you feel good about your progress on the Monarch project this week?" *(Closed-ended.)*

Questions about past performance

The whole point of establishing a critical incident file prior to beginning the CPR is to enable the manager to examine and discuss specific incidents. Questions about past performance draw on this data, and encourage discussion about specific events, rather than abstract precepts and ideas. Such questions allow you to discuss dates, people, times, places, names, and commitments.

- "Tell me what happened when . . . "

- "I'd be interested to hear how . . . "

You might elect to start with a past performance question highlighting a particular skill and/or event, and then probe further with question layering techniques:

- Who?

- What?

- Why?

- Where?

- When?

- How?

Handling incomplete or unclear answers

When you are dissatisfied with an answer or explanation or simply want to know more, try the one of the approaches below.

- "That's very interesting; tell me more about . . . "

- "Great; let's talk about another instance when . . ."

- "What other areas of _____ would you like to improve?"

Other useful "elucidating questions" would include:

- "Why do you say that?"

- "And then what happened?" or "What happened after that?"

- "How did that make you feel?"

- "What did you learn from this?"

Tone, body language, phrasing

At the same time you probe for information, you must make a conscious effort to be supportive of the employee. Your goal, after all, is to upgrade more employees than you weed out.

You can be supportive in three distinct ways.

1. By the way you listen and the body language you use.

2. By offering tangible help in the form of training and resources to help the employee grow.

3. Verbally, in the way you phrase statements and concerns.

The last of the three is perhaps the area most notably mishandled by managers during performance reviews. Consider the following comparisons.

- "You really screwed up on this one." *(Puts the worker on the defensive.)*

  "Something went wrong here; what do you think we can do to make sure it doesn't happen again?" *(Supportive.)*

- "Your performance is substandard." *(Antagonistic and overpersonalized.)*

  "Things haven't been progressing as well as either of us would like. How can I help us turn things around?" *(Concentrates on the positive and leaves room for the possibility of future improvement.)*

- "Shape up or ship out." (*An ultimatum without the offer of tools to change. Such a threat implies that the responsibility lies with the worker alone, and is in no way shared by the manager. Managers who use phrases like this are usually the same ones who blame every setback on an inadequate work force, only to later claim all the credit for their workers' achievements.*)

  "Let's agree on the areas we need to work on, the necessary tools, and the time we will need to make some headway." (*Reaffirms the worker/management partnership and the employee's sense of being part of the team.*)

- "You just never seem to listen to/understand instructions." (*An overaggressive generalization too vague to be of any real use.*)

  "I don't seem to be explaining my requirements on the Potter project in ways you can act on. What do you need from me to make things clearer here?" (*Specific, polite, and to the point.*)

- "Why don't you ever listen to what I tell you?" (*Less a question than a far-reaching, cynical accusation to which no self-respecting employee can make any reasoned response. If a worker doesn't seem to be listening or appears to have consistent problems in understanding something, the prudent manager, rather than pointing the finger of blame, will first imagine himself doing so . . . and realize that while one finger will be pointing out, three more will be pointing straight back at himself. Try to take responsibility for the miscommunication yourself.*)

  "It looks like I sent some mixed signals here; weren't we planning on doing . . . ?" (*May actually result in some constructive solution to the problem. Remember that*

*a manager's job is not to be right, but to get all the horses
in harness and pulling in unison.)*

Just as potentially threatening messages should be reformulated in a positive way, so must instances of inappropriate behavior be addressed as something other than inherent character defects.

You can't expect to improve matters with a tardy employee simply by informing him that he is "always late." Such a claim (if it is made at all) should at least be backed up with a review of expected start and finish times and specific dates and times of recorded transgressions. (The argument can be made that, in many cases, stating a negative in such stark fashion will only reconfirm the trait you want to reverse.)

The same applies to those workers who come in ten minutes late every day and leave ten minutes early to make up for it, and those who take advantage on the job by, for instance, starting lunch early and/or finishing it later than others. In such instances, telling someone that they are taking advantage is not as effective as explaining specifically which of their past activities you take exception to, complete with the relevant dates, times, and all other necessary incontrovertible facts.

WORKER COMMENTS

After all of the important dimensions have been probed, give the worker an opportunity to add anything else he feels is germane to the discussion. Theoretically, there should have been plenty of good communication on all the issues, but it is essential to give the employee one last chance to have his say before you proceed to the planning stages.

If you've done your preparation properly, you will reach agreement with the employee on the level of performance during the time period under discussion. If there is a problem, and you and the employee are still seeing things differently for some reason, use this stage to bridge the gap. Once you reach agreement, and not before, it's time to start planning for the future.

PLANNING

First of all, agree on the time lines.

> *"Well, Paul, let's decide when we will meet again; after that, we can agree on what we should be concentrating on until then."*

The all important planning phase will only be effective if everyone agrees and commits to the same schedule.

After you've established that, how do you determine what the person should shoot for?

"Do the best you can, Paul," is completely ineffective, of course. Even worse is to reach this point of the meeting and then adjourn without establishing any targets at all.

Your team members deserve clear, specific, measurable goals, and standards of performance. Ideally, the new targets should be moderately difficult but nevertheless readily achievable with a little effort. Overwhelm people with fear that they will never achieve your standards, and they will defeat themselves before they get off the starting block.

A good approach is to always ask the worker to set goals and performance standards; the groundwork for this was already laid in the last portion of the self-evaluation form. If the goals are realistic and agree with what you have determined as appropriate for the situation, all well and good. If not, you must negotiate either to raise or lower the achievement levels the employee identifies.

The plan you end up with should incorporate mutually defined benchmarks each party can watch for. When it comes to setting goals, small, achievable steps are preferable to impossible leaps into productivity heaven.

LOADED QUESTIONS

With specific upcoming or current projects in mind, you can ask the worker to focus on the matters at hand, and perhaps gain the opportunity to pass on good advice on avoiding snafus by asking a loaded question or two.

A loaded question is one that examines a current or anticipated event and examines how the worker is likely to handle it. You can form one by adapting either of the phrases below.

- "I'd be interested to hear how you plan to . . . (solve the problem with the XYZ account)."

- "What approach do you think you will take to . . . (the problems unearthed during the recent operational audit)?"

OF CARROTS AND STICKS

Rewards certainly can encourage a certain desired behavior, but individual rewards such as promotional, professional, or monetary incentives should only be used for those who are performing acceptably already. Used with those who don't fit into this category, such spoils may only win you a reputation as a manager who must bribe good performance out of subordinates. For this latter group however, you can use incentives such as books, seminars, audio and video training.

Stay away from unachievable incentives—whether for individuals or groups—at all times. Those contests offering the winner a six-month trip to the Bahamas for a 12,000% increase in productivity only fool the uninitiated once, but the ill will and distrust will linger for eons.

Agree on the areas to be targeted, and on how improvement in those areas will be achieved and judged by you both. Then determine what part each of you are expected to play in the day-to-day work world where these goals will be attained. Again, wherever possible have the employee offer his ideas in his words: don't dictate the terms.

WRAP-UP

With these commitments made, it is time to conclude the CPR meeting on a positive note. End the meeting as you would a regular selection interview: shuffle papers, change your position, stand up, smile, shake hands, and get on with business.

"WHO'S GOT TIME FOR ALL THIS?"

During my *Keeping the Best* seminars around the world, two distinctly different comments always arise with regard to CPRs.

The first comes from the person who has had some exposure to the idea of the critical performance review in the past. This manager invariably says something like, "Boy, that really drew blood: what you're talking about is one of the essentials of good management, but in the rush and rumble it's one of the things I've let slip. It's time I got back to the basics again."

The second viewpoint is expressed by someone who hasn't used the technique before: "Yeah, well, this all sounds really great . . . [pregnant pause] . . . in theory. But I don't have enough time as things stand; the last thing I want to do is add another mammoth review process with all its paperwork."

With the second group, I always try to get back to first causes.

The most valuable capital is human capital; the most powerful technology is people.

A manager's success is wholly dependent upon his ability to empower others.

Great work occurs only when managers and workers share each other's visions of the present and the future.

Shortcutting to avoid CPRs goes against all three of these fundamental precepts. It fools us into thinking that time spent on "all the things that have to get done" is more important than time spent with the people we expect to do them. It undercuts our efforts to understand and develop the aspirations of our employees. And it severely limits opportunities for pressure-free communication, a necessary component of job satisfaction.

Getting work done through others is a manager's job. Our performance is measured by how effectively we draw diverse personalities together and inspire commitment to common goals. While we understand that this is required of a manager to provide maximum return on investment for the company, we must also recognize that our employees only give what they get. Consider the return on investment from your subordinate's viewpoint as well as the company's.

It isn't so much that there isn't time to do CPRs as that there isn't time not to. So, how do we fit this new element into our schedules?

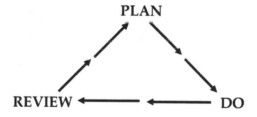

This is the simple Plan-Do-Review cycle that successful people in every field of endeavor all over the world do every day. Establish a set time every day to look at what went as planned, what needs adjustment, and what must be done to achieve our objectives tomorrow. Based on the review, make an action plan for the coming work period, implement it, and then complete the cycle by reviewing the results.

Incorporating CPRs into your routine might simply mean rearranging the day so that the review work replaces something else, or it might come in addition to all our other "perceived" hands-on tasks. I say "perceived" because we must always bear in mind that management is the job of empowering others with the skills and personal sense of responsibility to do the job without you. If you eventually have to delegate in order to work CPRs into your routine, so be it. Doing so is highly unlikely to lead to your working yourself out of a job.

Many managers find it effective to keep adjusted banker's hours; around 4:00, they close shop for the day and begin the review and planning process, which should include appropriate entries in the critical incident files. This approach also leaves time at the end of the day for necessary communications that will ensure coherence of efforts for the team on the following work day. However the issue is handled, the bottom line is that critical performance reviews should be an integral part of every manager's work week, either in preparing for them or in executing them.

THE SUPERIOR WORKER

I can't emphasize enough how important it is to meet with superior workers for performance evaluations. For those who rank eight or higher on a scale of ten, I recommend CPRs at least once a quarter. Too often we think that people who are doing well know as much, and know that we appreciate their efforts. Then it surprises us when they resign.

For these people, the CPR is a chance for one-on-one time with you and formal recognition of their efforts. Not only will CPRs serve as a powerful motivating force, drastically cutting down on those unexpected resignations—they will also help you justify raises and promotions when the time comes.

Every ninety days, feed back the results of your top members' CPR reviews to those who have formal or informal input on promotional procedures or fiscal advancement. Let them know about extra hours and special efforts that are put in by your best people. You can do this with a bald note stating the facts, or you can take the more subtle approach of providing strategic photocopies of memoranda illustrating X's special efforts over recent weeks. (In these instances, you might want to add a personalized note, jotted in the margin, specifying how much time or money was saved, or how much revenue generated, as a result of these initiatives. Your superiors won't always have the time to connect the dots; do it for them.)

There are other tactics you can use to promote these high performers, some of which extend beyond the formal reaches of the CPR. You might, for instance, get in the habit of delegating your everyday report-writing duties. Not only does this further develop team members, it also allows you (after appropriate editing) to leave their names on the report, which can then serve as a company billboard of sorts.

Don't leave your stars in departmental isolation. There are numerous meetings, standing committees, and task forces that occur during the year: bring key people to these proceedings. You may have to do some coaching as to the etiquette and professional presentation skills, but the effort will be worth it.

A consistent campaign that promotes your top people in this manner, when combined with the documentation provided by the ongoing CPR process, will make the justification of your wage and promotional suggestions that much easier. Furthermore, your generating strong performers carries the added plus of demonstrating what a damn fine manager you are, richly deserving of raises and promotions in your own right.

THE SATISFACTORY WORKER

The average and only just average workers, those in the five through seven range, may have the potential to achieve superior performance. A CPR schedule similar to those of the top contributors will help them realize that you care, and that you want them to achieve their personal and professional goals.

In this group, certain members may have one or two problem areas that need attention; in addition to your quarterly meetings, you might, for a period of time, institute more frequent CPRs with an eye to improving performance in specific areas.

Your goal throughout the process is not to maintain the level of performance these workers are achieving, but to bump them up into the next bracket. Stasis and dry rot (often euphemized as "steady" or "dependable" contribution) are no incentives to growth, and encouraging employee growth is, after all, the whole idea behind the CPR.

THE BELOW-AVERAGE WORKER

It is nothing short of alarming how readily many companies will hang onto long-term substandard employees for weeks, months, and even years, only letting them go in economic downturns when the economy provides an excuse to cut back on team strength.

Career ne'er-do-wells create motivational blocks for your best workers. Like it or not, peer pressure and the rule of the pack ultimately affect even the most motivated individuals. Few companies are completely immune from the risk of paralysis from inspired mediocrity. Holding our own isn't enough; it is necessary to trim away those who cannot contribute.

Simply by looking at those in your own organization at your level or higher, you can probably chart any number of borderline employees whose ascent toward the top of the organization is made possible by nothing other than the departure of more talented people. (And remember, talented people often leave because they feel "lumped in" with mediocre achievers.) Such an approach to climbing the corporate ladder is, while staid in the extreme, still probably the surest route to the top in most of our companies. Just as age is no guarantee of wisdom, longevity with a company is no accurate measure of ability. Longevity is rewarded so consistently, however, that one could be forgiven for assuming otherwise.

For the five-and-below group, you must demonstrate that there is one set of rules and standards for all. This is the group that will provide the most challenge and require the greatest time and effort. These employees may require weekly meetings or even more frequent contact. Stick to the program: with some of these workers, you will achieve gratifying, even inspiring improvements.

Still, no matter how good your intentions and how solid your efforts, some substandard employees will remain substandard regardless of how much time you spend with them. In these instances you have no alternative but to upgrade the staff, or, in other words, rid your organization of terminally poor performers.

Take heart: using the review procedures outlines in this chapter will help you to elevate the vast majority of your employees to acceptable levels of performance (at least). But when the day is done, you will probably still have to negotiate the departure of a number of intractable performance problems who will otherwise continue to pull down paychecks for no good reason at all.

Fortunately, you have other weapons at your disposal than outright, immediate dismissal. Frank calculations of performance (e.g., "I don't forsee any career growth for you here") are one weapon; biting the bullet and refusing to grant *any* pay increase when annual review time comes around is another. (Remember, we're talking about chronically inferior performers here.) If these methods fail, and you still find yourself supervising a bottom-of-the-barrel employee after, say, thirty days of "hardball" tactics, then it is probably time to part company.

If you don't want to, or think firing people is inhuman, consider this: you are a team coach, and when the team loses, management doesn't fire the team. It's the coach's head that rolls first.

Remember, if you fail to purge chronic poor performers, the best will either believe that you condone lackluster performance, or assume that you don't know the difference. Being the best, they will only want to associate with the best.

Avoiding the pain of firing an unimprovable employee may yield a staff with a low turnover rate, but it will leave only average and below-average performers. Your competition will get the best. Too often, companies and executives concerned about the turnover problem view the issue from a numbers and percentages viewpoint only: "Let's get turnover down from 18% to 7%." Clearly this is one issue where a quantitative approach is entirely inadequate. There are countless companies with low turnover and only marginal profitability. They have, by encouraging mediocrity in everything they do, served only to provide a dependable home for the lame and the halt of the corporate world.

Quick Summary of Key Concepts

- ✒ Slogans and/or increased quotas are generally ineffective in improving performance.

- ✒ Intelligently used, the critical performance review (CPR) can be a manager's most valuable productivity tool.

- ✒ Regular CPRs are not something to be restricted to substandard employees. The best team members will appreciate the feedback as much as anybody.

- ✒ Recognize good behavior and correct bad behavior, but be aware that everyone remembers criticism for far longer than praise.

- ✒ Discuss how current performance compares with established standards.

- ✒ Make sure the environment is conducive to two-way communication.

- ✒ Prepare for the CPR ahead of time.

- ✒ While CPRs will help improve many poorly performing employees, chronic, unimprovable problem workers must be weeded out.

Chapter Ten

Good Management Is Management That Listens

THE BEST EMPLOYEES COME IN VARIOUS SHAPES AND sizes, both sexes, and all colors. They come from all social, economic, and educational backgrounds.

Contrary to what many managers seem to believe, the best employees don't necessarily come with a Harvard Ph.D. attached. They can be found, and are desperately needed, at every rank of today's organizations. Learning to listen to them—and to the fellow workers we hope they will inspire—is often challenging, but it is essential if we are to build a super-competitive workforce.

DEGREES AS BARRIERS WITHIN THE ORGANIZATION

It is surprising how many of our companies' topmost people started out on the shop floor, considering that most of those same companies insist on advanced degrees for entry to the fast track. Calvin Coolidge's observation that our world is "full of educated layabouts" has been perhaps too easily forgotten, and the existing barriers to communication within our often-polarized organizations lead one to wonder whether or not the layabouts may have adopted a divide-and-conquer strategy.

Let's face it. In our dealings with employees, too much emphasis is placed on credentials alone, and not enough emphasis on a person's abilities and track record. (How many degreed incompetents have you run into over the years?)

Of course, credentials and job histories aren't always what they appear to be. It's estimated that at least three out of every ten resumes contain untruths, mostly to do with educational achievements, but sometimes veering into actual fictitious work experience.

We must reappraise the role of academic credentials in the communication and promotional processes of our organizations. This is not an argument for the election of high school dropouts to the board. The argument is, rather, that we climb out of our "need-to-know" rut and stop basing our communication in the workplace on standards that are neither meaningful nor just.

Consistently secretive "who-needs-to-know" judgments based on academics, title, or political leverage, beyond being wholly unnecessary in most cases, lead to a dangerous and self-fulfilling truism: most workers who put up with this eventually neither need nor want to "know."

Tomorrow's stars could be in lowly positions in the company today. We need to keep these workers just as much as we do the high flyers; foot soldiers count as corporate warriors, too. If we lose these "buck privates," we lose the strength that makes us great today, and the potential for our future greatness as well.

The best, it is worth repeating, can be found at all levels of our organizations. Moreover, the best want desperately to contribute; they have aspirations: sometimes to do the best job possible for a personal sense of self-worth, sometimes to do the best job possible to encourage their own professional growth, recognition, and respect.

When we tell a worker (through word or deed) that he has no right to know any more than is absolutely necessary for him to complete the narrow task he has been assigned, what we have really told him is that he is unworthy of such information, that he is incapable of making a difference in our organization. Under such a regime, most workers with a modicum of self-respect will choose to leave.

As Allstate's Donald Craib says, "Communications used to be way down on the average company's priority list. In many places it still is . . . (But we must recognize that, today,) employees are better educated. We're asking them to do more independent thinking. And they're asking for a better understanding, not just of what they are doing . . . but why they are doing it."

Contemporary management must ensure that it talks and listens effectively to everyone within the organization. This means not just immediate staff and the people in our own departments, but everyone with whom we come in contact. We have, in this way, defined what good corporate communication can and should be: giving and receiving input from all sources, regardless of status or rank, on an open and ongoing basis.

THE INNER COURT SYNDROME

Unfortunately most work units still function with an inner and an outer circle. The inner circle is blessed with an awareness of what's being undertaken; the outer circle operates in a void, effectively served with the significant demotivator of knowing that they are not "in the know."

This lack of communication is disabling in both directions. The inner circle is often insulated from real world experience and input because the outer circle is unable (and often unwilling) to offer ideas and express concerns to the inner circle. The outer circle becomes task-oriented rather than goal-oriented, and falls easily into a slipshod, disengaged workstyle. The bottom line: no cathedrals are built. This negative cycle often repeats itself throughout the diverse and overlapping work groups that exist in every company.

Good communication means the ability of the employee to affect the manager's thinking and actions, and vice versa. The objective is not to get the tail wagging the dog, of course, but to encourage the feeling of being heard, being listened to. When good communication is the order of the day, all parties come to feel that ideas, concerns, and suggestions are worthy of at least consideration.

Without such give-and-take, there is bound to be a certain troubling silence in the department. Directions may be accepted, and may even be executed, but they will not be executed with enthusiasm. Perhaps most damaging, directives will most likely be executed to the letter, although successful implementation requires execution to the spirit of the initiative as well. It is not uncommon for managers to have their directions consciously vandalized through overprecise, nothing-beyond-the-checklist campaigns instituted by demotivated subordinates. Many such managers never figure out exactly why things keep going wrong. Certainly, there is no incentive for anyone to tell them.

Too often, calcification sets in. The manager relies solely on the inner circle to get the job done when it is necessary to tackle the really challenging jobs. Together, the manager and the outer circle prove the manager's theories correct; the disenfranchised resign themselves completely to the status of second-class contributors. (But usually not for long. Such employees will leap at the chance to show their worth as a member of someone else's "inner circle.")

We can avoid this. All that is necessary is to affirm that if someone is worthy of working in our department they should, by the same token, be worthy of our confidence.

COMMUNICATION MEANS BEING UNDERSTOOD

We have already discussed how our workplace is changing. The male Caucasian is moving from being the majority stakeholder in the work force to being just another member of the plurality. Increasingly, our work force will include valuable team members for whom English is a second language; for whom the jargon of business approaches the status of an impenetrable foreign language; for whom our diverse corporate cultures are both strange and intimidating.

Yes, something as seemingly basic as language can be a major stumbling block to productivity. I have even known this issue to be the cause of union organization drives!

In 1979, over 40% of the work force at Bell Industries' Computer Memory Division in California came from other cultures. For some workers, English was a second language; for others it simply wasn't spoken at all. This was a time when the unions were banging with increasing vigor on Silicon Valley's doors. This division became a prime target, despite its having working conditions and benefits superior to those of most area companies, large or small.

The problem was language, pure and simple. It's no good providing a great place to work unless you understand the workers well enough to have some meaningful discussion with them about what is going to be done. The union people knew this; management was having a little trouble catching up.

Cliff Zachman, the divisional manager, spoke a little Spanish (the predominant first language), and had a solid reputation with a number of the workers as being trustworthy. Cliff understood it was impossible to insist the workers speak English only. Not only would this have been wildly optimistic, it would have inflamed the situation further. Instead, an effort was made on both sides: English classes for any who wanted them, and Spanish classes for those interested in learning that tongue. Later, a bilingual personnel director made a prominent commitment to personal growth for all employees, no matter what language they spoke. In short, the division provided tangible evidence of a company that cared. The unionization issue? It never came to a vote.

Copeland and Griggs, the San Francisco-based cultural diversity experts, point out that it would be supremely difficult for most of us to speak a second language all day, and offer these guidelines for dealing with the multicultural work force: "The English speakers must accept others' needs to speak in their own tongue, but most (of all), parties must make the conscious and consistent effort to let the others know what is being discussed, so that no individual or group feels alienated."

OPENING DIALOGUES, EXPANDING THE FOCUS

As more and more attention is paid to improving communication in the workplace, we see a healthy expansion of the issues and topics addressed by our companies. This expansion, which takes place as a result of listening to the concerns and needs of our workers, provides new and unique ways we can open dialogues and show our commitment to our people.

Honeywell's C.W. Johnson provides some examples:

> *Rape* is a four-letter word that we would not have mentioned in a business setting ten years ago, (yet) we have begun a new course on rape prevention, which is an acknowledgment that more and more of our women employees are travelling, working overtime and working in isolated locations.... We (also) had dialogue with a group of employees on affirmative action communications and practices, and have found the inputs invaluable in addressing this important subject.

Honeywell has subsequently developed additional programs to foster better understanding between men and women and blacks and whites in the workplace.

WHAT IT ALL MEANS

Mushroom management is dead, and its adherents are headed for the scrap heap. Effective management today requires communication, and entails operating with, as Ryder's Ron Dunbar puts it, "an open and above-board management style insisting that problems and decisions be openly discussed, and ensuring that employees are informed and involved as an integral part of the way they are managed."

Just as important, according to Allstate's Donald Craib, are "attitude, willingness to listen, respect for the individual's dignity: (these) are all part of a successful communications approach."

HOW TO GET THERE

You must plan to compensate for the wholly human tendency to place most importance on getting one's own message across. As the old (and accurate) adage has it, "No one ever really listens, we are all just waiting our turn to talk."

EFFECTIVE COMMUNICATION
IN THE WORKPLACE
IS A TWOFOLD TASK

The first essential is active listening. This fosters a spirit of openness. Our listening makes others want to communicate with us, and is the primary means by which we teach others to talk (or not to talk) to us.

The other essential is the sharing of information. This means giving instructions and posing questions, as well as discoursing on things at large.

LESSONS IN LISTENING

Listen to what the speaker has to say. Be open-minded. Even given the most approachable style of management, it is often difficult for many employees to screw up the courage to broach a sensitive topic with you. Sometimes the person's mode of expression will be at odds with the subject, perhaps even aggressive. Even the best blow their stacks from times to time, especially when they are nervous or frustrated. It bears repeating that frustration can be a good sign: it means the person cares enough to get a little worked up. It is your job to create an environment where frustrations can be aired and then channeled into productivity.

Make a valiant effort to see things from the other person's point of view. You might even try a little creative scriptwriting before a touchy meeting in an attempt to bring yourself closer to the mindset your worker will bring to the discussion.

Stay calm, even if the person's tact is not all it could be. Good managers develop the ability to pick out the message the speaker is trying to communicate, and don't confuse the information with how the person is expressing himself.

If the employee speaks a great deal in terms of "I" and "me," this usually means he is searching for recognition, personal validation, and a sense of self-worth. If the employee talks about "they" or "the others," he is likely trying to distance himself from a position or action he disagrees with. It takes careful listening to understand a person's point of view and motivation, but doing so almost always yields new insights and ideas. Listening well has one other benefit: it builds a sense of obligation in the other person to listen to you when it is your turn to speak.

Listening: body language

We are seen to be listening and empathizing not only through remaining silent as our partner speaks, but primarily through our body language. Often, managers send workers discouraging body signals without even knowing it.

What is the point of sitting quietly if our body language is loudly proclaiming our disagreement, our boredom, or our ambivalence? Negative body signals include shaking the head, sighing, looking at one's wristwatch or out of the window, yawning, sitting back and folding arms and crossing legs, and, of course, the oh-so-eloquent habit of staring determinedly at the ceiling as if to say, "Why me, Lord?"

These are all guaranteed to make the speaker defensive, or, worse still, convince him to stop trying to communicate with us at all. The best way to avoid sending such inappropriate messages is to be aware of what we are doing with our bodies and minds in these situations.

Another sure-fire way to avoid negative body language is to make sure that the feedback you do give with your body is positive. Smile, keep eye contact, nod, and make encouraging "mm hm" sounds at appropriate intervals. Actively encourage the employee to talk more with phrases like:

- "That's interesting; tell me more."

- "Great; give me another example."

- "Why do you say that?"

- "And then what happened?"

- "What do you think caused this?"

- "How does that make you feel?"

- "What have you learned from all this?"

These are simple phrases that show you are interested in what the speaker is saying. At the same time, these conversational tools give you greater insight into what the speaker is experiencing.

THE TRANSITION

There is a natural tendency to offer one's response to the speaker's comments once he has stopped speaking, but beware: by doing so you will be skipping a small but vital confirmation step.

All you really should do at this stage is make sure you heard and understood what the other person was really saying. To this end, use your chance to speak by verifying what you have just been told.

- "In other words, you feel that . . ."

- "OK; what I'm getting is . . ."

- "So if I hear you correctly, what you are saying is . . ."

Using this technique assures the speaker that you have really been paying attention, and offers an opportunity for clarification.

GETTING YOUR MESSAGE ACROSS

Of course, once you have clarified the nature and intent of your speaker's message, you will want to be sure your own message is delivered in a clear and comprehensible manner.

As you frame your response, remember that whatever behavior you choose to give attention to is the behavior you will reinforce. Avoid negatively phrased statements: "You made a mistake." Emphasize instead your commitment to ongoing growth: "What would be a better way to for us to tackle this?" (You may want to review the earlier discussion of positive phrasing in the chapter on critical performance reviews.) Focus on praise and encouragement, but be careful not to give one when the other is due.

Encouragement indicates that you are paying close enough attention to recognize small victories as necessary mileposts on the long road to competence, achievement, and success. Encouragement shows that you are cheering on your players as any good coach would. Encouragement demonstrates that you have faith and confidence in your team and in their will to win.

Praise, on the other hand, is far more sparingly given. Praise is always won with effort. Praise recognizes attainment of a goal. Praise is a metaphorical clap on the back for a job well done.

Praise is the recognition without which workers mutter, "Why bother; no one ever notices anyway."

Issuing praise that has not been earned demonstrates only that you either aren't paying attention or are incapable of distinguishing genuine achievement from busy work. False praise, in the end, is no better at motivating workers than blind neglect is.

IN THE KNOW

Remember, no one wants yesterday's news. Being in the know means getting the knowledge when it is fresh and relevant, not when it is nine days old.

The knowledge you share can be packaged in terms of how the information affects your people, their goals, and the commitments of your department or work group. Tie personal and group goals together during this packaging process, and the communication battle is half won. Some managers take a more hands-off approach, however, and simply have a revolving file, into which everything relevant they receive is put. The file remains in constant circulation around the department.

Regular meetings also play an important role; they allow knowledge to circulate and encourage perceptual exchanges between the people who will subsequently make things happen. Unfortunately, meetings have a way of biting into productive prime time. To avoid this, you can schedule them first thing in the morning, which helps ensure that the gang is all there on time. Another great slot is right before twelve noon. It is nothing short of amazing how much ground can be covered in the five or ten minutes before lunch; for some mysterious reason, man's attraction to buck-passing and doubletalk recedes dramatically every day during these few moments. (Meeting times that encourage brevity also keep interest levels high.)

COMMUNICATION MEANS CREDIT

Your effectiveness as a communicator is based not just on what you say as a result of careful listening, but also on what you do.

After soliciting input, make a visible effort to act on it and credit its source. It is counterproductive to solicit good input from team members, then put it into action with no accreditation (or, worse still, with incorrect accreditation).

Here are some other useful ideas on this score:

- Praise creative ideas whenever you hear them; you will encourage innovation and success-oriented thinking.

- Recognize achievements publicly; express your confidence and pride in the achiever publicly.

- Accentuate the positive to build positive behavior. It cannot be repeated often enough: whatever behavior you recognize will be reinforced. Handle any substandard or inappropriate behavior in private. Respect the person's sense of dignity; make any criticism constructive.

- Always explain the thinking behind your decisions, and the reasons for your following a particular course. Acknowledge the influence of your team's input.

- Share experiences—both successes and failures—with your people. It is tremendously motivating for those who work for you to see how you have suffered setbacks and bounced back.

- Admit to being wrong once in a while. Like it or not, you do make mistakes, and your employees know it. They can't chew you out for screwing up, and that can cause resentment. Admitting error once in a while shows objectivity, and encourages others to display the same attractive trait.

THE OPPORTUNITY TO CONTRIBUTE

Company-wide emphasis on good communication affords all employees, regardless of rank, the opportunity to contribute. The feeling that one's opinion counts in the grand scheme of things provides an enhanced sense of self-worth, and people who feel good about themselves because of the work they do will in turn feel good about the employer who makes this possible.

Quick Summary of Key Concepts

ε&. When we tell a worker (through word or deed) that he has no right to know any more than is absolutely necessary for him to complete the narrow task he has been assigned, what we have really told him is that he is unworthy of such information.

ε&. Contemporary management must ensure that it talks and listens effectively to everyone within the organization.

ε&. The "inner court syndrome" leads to a polarized and ineffective work force.

ε&. Effective communication in the workplace is a twofold task. The first essential is active listening; the other is the effective sharing of information.

ε&. Good managers develop the ability to pick out the message the speaker is trying to communicate, and don't confuse information with how the person is expressing himself.

ε&. Often, managers send workers discouraging body signals without even knowing it.

ε&. Good managers use both their failures and their successes as valuable communication and training tools.

Chapter Eleven

Delegation
Breeds
Commitment

INCREASINGLY, AS RECOGNITION OF WORTH AND reward for effort cannot be repaid with the standard means of reward—promotion—the modern manager, intent on keeping the best, must use delegation of responsibility and authority as a means of repayment and to encourage career growth. The results, in terms of job satisfaction, can be quite spectacular. Employees come less and less to feel like automatons carrying out instructions mindlessly, and more and more like productive members of a team.

THE PARADOX

We ascend to the hallowed ranks of management by virtue of superior personal capabilities and achievements, but on reaching the holy of holies we are immediately faced with a cruel paradox. Although promoted in recognition of outstanding personal performance, we are now told to accomplish even more, and, ideally, to do so without performing any of the tasks ourselves. The transition from direction-taker to direction-issuer is often a rough one indeed.

Unfortunately, this transition from implementation to facilitation is one that only a fraction of managers ever completely master, sometimes despite decades on the job. This may be because the great majority of companies still do not have formal management training programs, substituting on-the-job training instead. This leads us to the corporate world's dirtiest secret, namely that the majority of our managers have never received any kind of formal management training at any stage of their career.

If we accept that the first tenet of management is to get work done through others, then we must commit to enhance management capability in two basic ways: by encouraging effective delegation and through the development of training skills. In this chapter, we will examine the fundamentals of delegation; training will be covered in the next chapter.

DELEGATION: CORNERSTONE TO COMMITMENT

In recent years, we saw a great influx of inexperienced workers; jobs were made small and numerous layers of management were justified to give adequate supervision to new and inexperienced workers. Now these workers have hit the top of their stride and are looking to stretch and make their mark. The result? We will have to build challenge and stretch back into jobs for the experienced worker and provide equal scope for the younger generation now snapping at their heels.

As Peter Drucker says in *Frontiers of Management*, "Now we have to structure jobs so that the young people ask, 'What can I do to make the job bigger, more challenging, more achieving, more rewarding?' And we will have to learn again that recognition, both through money and through other means, has to motivate to improve performance on the job."

Once we accept that arrival on Mahogany Row means doing less of what got us there, we can begin to get our super-competency thrills vicariously, bringing others up to superior levels of performance and increasing their sense of personal achievement. If we do not use delegation as a tool in this way, we will suffer professionally. Our future promotional opportunities will diminish as our own management loses faith, our employees work against us, and, eventually, we burn out.

As managers, we often hold an innate belief in our own superiority: "If you want a job done well, you have to do it yourself." But is it a short- or long-term "job done well" that we are after? Effective delegation by its very nature entails allowing for the possibility of failure in a controlled environment. People learn best from experience, and the best experience is still to learn from your own mistakes.

The specter of insecurity also ranks high on the list of obstacles to the acceptance of delegation. While most managers recognize intellectually the rule that advancement requires the presence of an able successor, a good percentage simply pay this idea lip service. "What if Ellen is really as good as I think she is? I could be signing my own death warrant!"

There are, of course, more rational fears of delegation. Many managers have bad experiences with it. The horror stories tend to come in two varieties. The first is fairly straightforward: "I tried it once and it was an embarrassment; eventually, I had no choice but to do it myself." The second major class of delegation failure is a little more complex. Many companies do ask their managers to experiment and be creative in job assignments, but are quick to punish the slightest failure. The message gets around quickly: it is far safer to talk about modern management than actually get involved with it.

In addition, there are still some race- and gender-based hurdles with regard to delegation. As we saw earlier, there are often unspoken (and perhaps unconscious) efforts to "protect" minority employees from challenges that are seen, somewhat condescendingly, as being too stiff. The result is that the employee is denied the enriching experience of failure. Accordingly, minority employees often feel they must "pitch a perfect game" every time out just to get access to the same chances everyone else has.

WHAT DELEGATION ISN'T

To be truly successful as managers, then, we must overcome such obstacles and work to set up an effective delegation environment. Before we can do so, however, we must make an objective evaluation of the existing climate. Delegation will never flourish if our relationships and knowledge of our workers is limited to their names and weaknesses.

Delegation certainly isn't spending the day stuffing envelopes right along with the troops; neither is it long hours spent in motivational psychobabble meetings in hopes of wheedling our people into doing what we have asked.

Make the tasks you delegate meaningful. The tasks you delegate should be both challenging and attainable. Watering the office plants, for instance, doesn't fit into the meaningful category.

SOME WARNING SIGNS

A good indication of one's delegation ability is the height and age of the contents of your in-box. Are piles of work regularly dragged home at night or over weekends? Are days spent mainly rushing to put out fires and direct rear guard containment actions?

Take a few moments to go over the following checklist. How many of these problems are sniping at your back?

- You can't take time off, even when you are sick and close to death's door, because there is no-one capable of pinch-hitting for you.

- You are never able to take all the vacation time you have coming.

- You aren't able to set aside at least 30 minutes for planning at a set time every day.

- You must frequently help workers finish their projects.

- Your subordinates lack initiative. They can't seem to turn around without feeling they must ask permission. (Of course, they can't be trusted too far anyway.)

- Getting information from team members is always like pulling teeth.

- If you left, the company would have to hire from outside for a replacement.

- Effective delegation is not a criteria for management performance evaluations in your company.

A DELEGATION PLAN

There are some wonderful managers who delegate, but only on special occasions—like when a tough project comes their way. The thinking: "Oh, boy: this one looks dangerous. Well, I'm not winding up with the egg on my face. Anyway, the boss is always talking about how important delegation is." This isn't delegating, this is dumping.

Remember when you delegate that, although you pass on both responsibility and authority, the action never relieves you of either. The buck still stops at your desk. Delegation is the tool prudent managers use to fulfill obligations successfully, not to duck them.

A modern manager must be seen to be in command, with the ability to both plan courses of attack and allocate resources for the coming battles. However, we face something of a catch-22 situation here: we can only achieve the time to plan courses of attack and allocate resources if we delegate effectively.

Creating time to clear the decks to plan and monitor delegation projects within the department is a manager's greatest asset.

Delegation is the way a successful manager boosts personal productivity by, in essence, multiplying himself.

In discussing critical performance reviews, we looked at the essential management cycle:

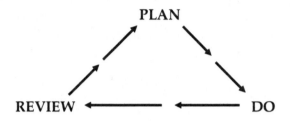

We can adapt it to our delegation needs, as well.

The planning portion of the cycle is where you evaluate the events likely to arise from different courses of delegation, and examine the effects of different combinations of your resources, human and otherwise.

The doing portion of the cycle includes the actual organizing and directing. Here, you create the environment where your team members can learn and achieve, allowing workers to make decisions within a predetermined area rather than just carry out instructions. They will make mistakes; that is not at issue. What matters is how you deal with those mistakes.

The review portion of the cycle is that time you allot during the day to look back and evaluate. Who did well? Who needs assistance? What form should that assistance take? This portion segues into the next planning portion, as you move toward creating blueprints for the next day.

DELEGATION IN ACTION

Effective delegation requires taking a long perspective. Seeing that the job is done properly, of course, is our responsibility as managers, yet full development of the team is equally important. The most qualified person for a particular job may not be the one who will benefit from it most, and often is by no means the most motivated. Assign growth-oriented tasks bearing in mind the fundamental principles. *The most valuable capital is human capital; the most powerful technology is people.*

Once a leader for the project has been chosen, set up feedback and communication procedures. Be sure to spend enough time on this aspect: once the task has been delegated, you should have minimized the natural tendency to peer over the worker's shoulder continually.

You can increase your chances for success when you ask yourself these questions before a new delegation opportunity is assigned:

- What results are you expecting? (Include dates, times, places, dollars, and percentages wherever relevant.)

- Who will be involved peripherally?

- With what frequency will benchmark meetings take place?

- How will success or failure be assessed?

- What specific materials and resources must be made available to maximize the chances of success? (And what role can the chosen team member/members play in this resource allocation?)

- What is the deadline for the job? (Must the worker/ workers have an ability to work under pressure?)

- How much communication/feedback/direction will be necessary for the project? (How does this affect A's suitability for the job over B's?)

- Who will benefit most from the experience?

- How will the chosen project leader complement the overall strengths of the work group?

- To what extent does the person under consideration seek out new challenges in the regular course of events? (Note, however, that with our increasingly diverse work force we must take into account that some cultures do not encourage forwardness and self-promotion. Failing to take this into account may lead us to make the mistake of overlooking otherwise promising minority candidates.)

- How competent is the person at regular duties? (If someone is still struggling to master basic responsibilities, it is in no one's interest to offer more challenges until the employee is ready for them.)

- How effective are the person's written and verbal communication skills? (Assigning important tasks to subordinates requires that you confirm there is a basic proficiency here; you must be able to gather the information necessary to gauge progress and make decisions about the ultimate outcome of the assignment.)

- Is the person organized enough to keep important details from falling through the cracks? If not, could the assignment be used as an exercise to turn this particular weakness into a strength? (Whenever an assignment is used in this way, be sure to let the worker know that there is an additional goal to the assignment. It is also imperative to provide tools necessary to give the employee a reasonable chance of success.)

- Will the assignment require working alone or interaction with others?

- If there is interaction with others, will it be within the department or interdepartmental?

- If interdepartmental, will there be any potential communication problems with others of different levels in those departments? (Try to identify steps you can take now to ensure a fruitful experience for all concerned.)

- Is the assignment predictable—with clearly defined parameters and clear steps to completion—or is a certain creativity required to bring it to fruition?

After defining the task and choosing the lucky devil who's going to carry it out, it is time to get the train out of the station. Sit down with the worker in question; let him know what the task is and what's expected by way of results. A brief outline of the objective and the desired outcome is enough to get the conversation started. In effect, the delegation starts now: let the assignee give the major input on the hows and whens of completion. It is also preferable to allow project leaders to set deadlines in conference with you, rather than impose them from above.

LETTING GO

Once you are committed to an assignment and a person to complete it, step back and give the employee elbow room. It is self-defeating to give someone the responsibility for a project's completion, but withhold the authority necessary to do the job. Announce the assignment and the responsible parties, and introduce the parties involved wherever necessary (i.e., to any out-of-department people involved with the project). Give your employee your public backing.

Regardless of how sorely you may be tempted, don't stick your nose in. Review progress only at the predetermined times. You can, of course, act as cheerleader whenever you see an opportunity, expressing your confidence in the undertaking's successful conclusion. Remember at all times, however, that the project is not yours to complete.

There is a delicate balance between leaving the job to the individual and abandoning them to the winds of fate. While the work may well be out of your hands, it should never be out of your mind. Certainly, it is asking for trouble to ignore an assigned project for too long (especially if both you and the subordinate are new to delegation). Outright neglect, in fact, is a good indicator of an insecure manager who doesn't *want* delegation to work, who is actually only waiting for the fire alarms to ring through the halls. This way, he can rush to the scene of the disaster, issuing Mighty Mouse's triumphant cry: "Here I come to save the day!"

If the project leader experiences difficulties, you can ask what assistance you can offer, as long as you follow a simple rule: you ask the questions, the employee comes up with the answers. If things get really rough, let your subordinate know that you didn't expect it to be an easy job, and that this is why he was chosen: because you knew he could handle it. Such encouragement is often of more help in a delegation situation than actual advice.

Whatever you do, don't go rushing into that burning building half asleep with your PJs flapping. Resist the urge to snatch back the responsibility and authority in an effort to return things to an even keel. Step back and review the situation. Perhaps the problem is in the parameters of the task itself or the benchmarks you have set for feedback. You may even need to take a long hard look at your leadership/delegation style.

The only time direct intervention is justified is when the department or your professional reputation could suffer significant setbacks if you do not step in. If poor quality or serious deadline crises seem unavoidable, you may well have to take a more active role, but do so as a last resort. Only when the ship is heading directly for the rocks do you need to set up frequent joint working sessions where both you and the subordinate are involved with the generation of a suitable end result. This is difficult for every manager, but remember your overall goal: increasing the self-sufficiency of your team members. In such cases (they should be quite rare), you can still concentrate on helping the project leader solve the problem rather than providing the solution yourself.

Do whatever it takes to get the job finished with a semblance of the delegation still intact. Abandoning delegation completely will advertise flaws in your management style and abilities. It is only after the project is completed that you should come to decisions about the nature and complexity of future projects for this particular person or group.

When there are problems with delegation, your consideration should always be along these lines:

- "How can I make X more successful next time?"

- "How can I improve my management style to make delegation more effective?"

Delegation itself should never come under question, unless you are tired of the responsibilities of management.

Quick Summary of Key Concepts

▪ As recognition of worth and reward for effort increasingly cannot be repaid with the standard means of reward—promotion—the modern manager must use delegation of responsibility and authority as a means of repayment and to encourage career growth.

▪ Arrival on Mahogany Row means doing less of what got us there.

▪ We must overcome any resistance to delegation we may feel, whether this resistance is based in insecurity or past problems in execution.

▪ The most appropriate person for a particular job may not be the most qualified. Often, the most qualified person is not the most motivated.

▪ Once a leader for the project has been chosen, set up proper feedback and communication procedures.

▪ Avoid the temptation to abandon the delegation process when there are problems; allowing people to make mistakes within predetermined parameters is the best way to encourage meaningful growth.

Chapter Twelve

Training: Opportunities to Grow and Excel

WE HAVE ALREADY SEEN THAT OUR MOST IMPORTANT resource is people. It follows logically enough, then, that if we spend money to keep our machines maintained well, we owe at least as much to our employees at all levels.

Many current management theorists, as we noted earlier, applaud the idea of developing the company hero: the star, the superperformer who towers above his peers and rockets to the top of an organization. This approach, in my view, is short-sighted. Considering the intense competition for skilled workers—competition that is, as we have seen, only going to intensify—the charismatic beneficiaries of carefully orchestrated succession plans may well show up for work one morning and find there is no one left to inspire.

Although it is certainly important to develop the leaders who will guide our corporate fortunes through the end of the century, it just as important is to keep the rest of our corporate warriors at all levels committed and motivated, and one proven way to do that is through ongoing training.

Those invaluable people who come in just a notch below the "trumpeter swans" and the "champions" offer a wellspring of potential that we can either take advantage of or ignore. If we choose the path of ignoring them, we do so at our own peril. These are the loyal corporate warriors who, with sweat and dedication, allow the stars to shine and the company to prosper. They too must be nurtured if we are to achieve the highest levels of success.

For the sad fact is that we are in no real danger of running out of chiefs, but are in grave danger of running out of good corporate warriors. The developed countries now need brain labor—not brute force—yet that potential work force is shrinking alarmingly. Many entry-level workers simply do not have the essential basic reading, writing, and computational skills to serve business needs over the coming years.

In an address to the Literacy Council, Chrysler vice president Richard E. Acosta acknowledged a new and alarming statistic, noting recent estimates that U.S. industry spends something on the order of $25–30 billion a year to train poorly schooled workers. There is an old bromide to the effect that if you think education is expensive, you should check the price tag on ignorance. It is becoming more and more difficult to dismiss.

RAISING THE STANDARDS

The young men and women coming out of our schools, then, need better basic skills to compete and contribute in today's world. And for the increasing number of older workers we anticipate in the work force, we must often provide skills that are now taken for granted but that may not have been taught, learned, or perhaps did not even exist in their schooling days. At the 1988 Conference on the Aging Work Force, Robert Stempel of General Motors put it in a nutshell: "The old idea of education as something that ended once you started working is worse than useless, and people who cling to it will be left behind."

This view is shared by James Boswell, vice president of employee relations at the *Los Angeles Times*. "Not only will the more educated worker demand the right to learn," Boswell predicts, "but larger numbers of employees will also require retraining and updating of skills as their jobs become more technologically oriented." In short, the days when rewarding jobs required little more than a willingness to work hard, but few formal skills, have, for all practical purposes, passed. If only for the sake of survival, students, parents, educators, management, labor, and federal and state government must join together and make a sustained effort to improve educational standards.

In a speech to the University of Chicago Business School, Xerox chairman David Kearns put the cost of finding the right people and keeping them at $210 billion a year, a figure incorporating both formal and informal job training.

Some companies do go to almost-unbelievable lengths to span the skill gaps left by the rapidly changing world and our substandard educational system. Xerox, for example, has found that training its own people isn't always enough, and has gone so far as to begin training its suppliers. Others go even further: Motorola trains its suppliers' suppliers.

While this isn't practical for all of us, there is a valuable lesson to be learned: employee training is an essential tool we will need to use more and more in the coming years. We live in a time when lifelong learning is the order of the day. As David Kearns puts it, "Business will need people who have learned how to learn, because working and learning are becoming inseparable."

Training empowers people. And because we all enjoy doing the things we do well, training leads to a happier, healthier and more productive work force. After all, things only get accomplished above and beyond our expectations when people enjoy doing them. When our people are happy, well trained, and committed, they will stick by us loyally and give us their all.

The needs for training in any given corporation are endless. At Intel, a world leader in chip technology, they have an interesting three-pronged approach that I think is worth emulating. It looks like this:

- Straightforward skill training

- Success training

- Diversity training

Straightforward skill training

Skill training addresses the functional developmental needs of all levels of employees: not just the highest levels of management and the technical ranks, but also the clerical and support people.

Considering the high-tech orientation of the company, it is remarkable how much thought and effort goes into Intel's support of its clerical people. Here is what Dr. Bonnie Johnson, Intel's manager of office systems development, has to say about the training needs of the clerical work force when it comes to word processing: "We have evidence which shows that you must invest as much in learning as you invest in equipment. In W.P., that is about $1000 per person. That is about what a personal computer costs; that is (also) about what continuous learning costs."

Intel's clerical workers get membership in an ongoing educational program, with training opportunities arising perhaps twice a month. Johnson places great importance on continuous training. "A major reason some people are resistant to technology," she notes, "is fear: not of the technology itself, but of being stranded. We made a commitment to the operators to support them, and we found that as long as people think they are not going to be stranded, they will use the equipment—and their job satisfaction will increase."

Success training

Intel's leadership is a golden example of management that acknowledges that an employee is by nature more eager to fulfill his own goals than those of the corporation. Management also knows, however, that once the two can be brought into alignment, both parties will benefit and prosper.

The corporation, through its many career development programs, gives every sign of being eager to fulfill productive employee aspirations. Intel provides training in the areas of corporate culture and requirements for success, as well as such thoughtful programs as how specific career choices will affect one's advancement. The intent is that Intel employees will at least know what it takes to get where they want to go.

Diversity training

According to San Francisco's Lewis Griggs, Intel began a series of multicultural integration workshops for Chinese employees several years ago, then extended the program to East Indians and Pakistanis. The firm now offers specialized training and career planning programs to all foreign-born employees.

The diversity training programs teach participants cross-cultural communication skills and point out potential stumbling blocks. They include such programs as "How to get ahead in an American company," personalized coaching in English language skills, and what they term "moving up " classes—the integration of U.S. and Intel culture, as it applies to a successful corporate career. Do you think the beneficiaries of such programs develop any deep-seated loyalty to the company?

All this is still more evidence of a firm that thinks first and foremost of its employees, puts its money where its mouth is, and wins commitment and dedication as a result.

Mere talk of motivation is cheap, of course; results are what counts. And, by that measure, one concludes that Intel is a world leader in its market, thanks in large part to its advanced technology. But by that I do not necessarily mean circuit boards and computer chips. I mean, first and foremost, *people*. The commitment and contributions of its people at all levels have earned Intel a well-deserved reputation as a place where men and women can achieve their goals, and can do so in an environment where they know their contributions will be appreciated.

PRACTICAL ASPECTS OF TRAINING

As we reevaluate ongoing training and accept its mandatory role in the contemporary workplace, we must also reevaluate our own training skills and philosophies.

The guiding principles of the bad old days are easy to spot from a distance: "Here, read this manual," or "Here, watch me; OK, that's how you do it, now get on with the job." A somewhat more systematic approach is in order if we are to reap all the benefits of a good training program.

GETTING THE TRAINEES RIGHT

The right training for the task at hand must be preceded by the proper selection of the people to be trained. Such a point may seem self-evident, but consider the following cautionary tale from Emhart's Marion S. Kellogg concerning proper installation of a robot in an industrial environment.

> We did all the right things . . . We helped the factory organization select the robot, made sure they got the right one, and helped them buy it. We looked at the application; we were pretty sure it was going to work. We brought the robot in and debugged it. Then we brought in all the hourly workers who were going to maintain it, along with those who preceded the robot in the line and those who followed the robot in the line, so that they all understood how the robot worked and exactly what their role would be.

> Well, the people who came to be trained were on top of the world. When they went back their jobs, they were kings. They knew things that other people didn't know. They loved the robot . . . they named it Tillie. They drew a face in it, and would pat it as they went by. It really was a splendid experience . . .

About ten weeks later, however, a team was sent to do the follow-up and perhaps get some shots for publicity. This was, after all, a great example of training at its best. What did they find?

> When we got there, the robot was (hidden away) in the corner. It was not functioning. It was covered in dust, unused.

> It wasn't the union (that had taken the robot off line, as we'd initially suspected) . . . it was the foreman. The foreman had

never been trained; (suddenly) his men knew more than he did.

And, apparently, he didn't like that one bit!

The moral: training is never completely effective unless all affected parties are involved. However, while this is an easy enough principle to set down on paper, implementing it can be a challenge.

The general attitude toward training in most of our companies is itself a major stumbling block. Take applicant interviewing, for instance. Eight out of ten managers have never been taught how to interview effectively. Typically, the two that have been were taught to do so only after entering the ranks of management.

And so it is with the other learned skills of the management team. If taught at all, they tend to be taught after the fact, when someone is already in the driver's seat, causing who knows what sort of damage to commitment and productivity.

Better that these and other professional enhancement skills be offered on an elective basis prior to promotions, so that, in effect the career-driven select themselves for growth with the effort and commitment they display before the fact.

ELECTIVE TRAINING

While at many company or association conventions (the occasions where most training gets done) there is an exclusive management track, here and there we are seeing some dramatic changes. Instead of a restricted management training track, meetings are increasingly open to all interested parties. In other words, those committed and career-oriented professionals you hope to develop can further their own careers by learning new skills at elective sessions populated by employees of many ranks, rather than attending the same narrow sessions geared only to people with their titles.

Offering elective training for employees also allows the best some much-needed visibility. In most cases, all that is necessary is to make all training available to all who express an interest; you can then take your cue from the employees who demonstrate their commitment.

Some of the larger companies have formalized this procedure and have, in the process, passed along some interesting lessons. Take aerospace giant McDonnell Douglas; they have something called a "high potential program" designed to identify and encourage high-potential employees, or HiPots for short. By offering recognition and providing access to the tools of achievement, the company aims to keep its best fulfilled and committed.

The program, largely the work of McDonnell Douglas's Mary Suttle, offers a limited number of slots. Employees are encouraged to nominate themselves, and are expected to justify their nomination along strict guidelines. Applicants must outline a five-to-ten-year development plan that outlines career objectives, previous accomplishments, formal and informal training, educational attainments, and professional accreditation, recommendations from both the management and peer group, and copies of performance reviews. (Such daunting requirements do a good job of weeding out the "Yeah, sure, I'll take some time off for training" crowd.)

A specially elected committee reviews the proposals. "Greatest weight (is) given to the proposal itself," according to Suttle. "Did the applicant clearly define where he or she wanted to be five years from now? Given that objective, did the applicant define the development steps necessary?"

Not only does elective training make good sense economically, it convinces employees they work for a company that wants them to succeed. And as employees ourselves, isn't this exactly what we look for in an employer?

KEYS TO EFFECTIVE TRAINING

Whatever topic you are training, whatever the size of the group, there are some common methodologies that will enhance your presentation. By following the guidelines set out below, you will maximize impact and retention and go a long way toward making the experience an enjoyable one for the participants.

Focus on the topic

All good training sessions start with an explanation of the topic to be discussed, as well as a discussion of how the presentation will help the trainees to be more successful in their work. Appealing to vague procedural goals is a sure way to lose people, but giving examples of how what you have to say will help the listener achieve his own goals will win attention.

Set the ground rules

Explain start and finish times, break times, and the like; this gives participants a framework within which to learn. Make a point of encouraging questions and explaining how they will be handled.

In my seminars and workshops on employee selection and motivation, I always take a moment to clarify this issue. The rundown sounds like this:

> Any question is a good question, and this session can only be as good as the effort you put into it. I want you to feel free to ask any question at any time. I will handle your question in one of three ways. My preference is to answer it then and there, but if you raise a topic we will be addressing later in the program, I will explain this and ask you to hold the question until that time. It is also possible that you might have a great question that, while valid, doesn't quite fit into the content and time constraints of this program. In this instance I'll also ask you to hold the question—until a break—so we can discuss it in detail one on one.

Liven it up

Like it or not, we live in an age in which television and the movies have dramatically affected the way we learn. Attention spans are much shorter than they once were; the presentation that does not take this into account will suffer as a result.

Think television. Most television programs are divided into segments, few lasting more than eighteen minutes. Experience has proven that after this point there is a mental break; proceeding beyond the eighteen-minute border means risking serious lapses in your audience's attention. Programming executives can't take that risk, and neither should you. Build suitable breaks into your training in keeping with the eighteen-minute rule.

Sometimes this will be a simple coffee break (you need one at least every ninety minutes). Apart from this type of break, changing the pace or training style—from, say, straight presentation to video—should refresh minds and regain attention.

Perhaps you have been lecturing for eighteen minutes; now would be a good time to break the audience up into informal discussion groups. It doesn't matter that you are the expert and you have more to say. Continuing to rattle on for another ten minutes will only get people shifting uneasily in their seats. If you want to get the message across, incorporate variety to your presentation.

Many programs consist simply of speeches delivered from a podium for an hour and a half or so—the old standard of boredom. Most of the rest conform to the new standard of boredom: speeches from a podium in a darkened room while an endless series of 35mm slides are projected onto a screen.

If you adhere to either of these methods, your company training programs are not getting their messages across nearly as forcefully as they might. Of course, it may be difficult for us to take a long hard look at programs on which we've labored mightily and admit that they are less than compelling in their delivery. Yet unless we want to prompt waves of absent-minded doodling (or worse, outright snores) it must be done.

Three steps

When teaching a new skill, whether it be using a new form or tapping hidden powers of self-motivation, your program design should incorporate three distinct steps for best retention.

Step one: I tell you; I demonstrate; you watch and listen.

Step two: You tell me; we do it together; we discuss the pros and cons.

Step three: You do it; I watch and listen; we discuss it.

THE WAY WE LEARN

Training can yield impressive rewards from the first moment: employees know that training is an important part of receiving raises and promotions or higher commissions. In addition, the mere act of involving the employee in training usually serves to demonstrate vividly that he is a competent, recognized, and valued member of the team. (Training that is obviously "remedial" in nature may be the exception here, but even then the company's investment in the employee as a person comes across.) Effective training captures and holds the trainee's attention. It provides the confidence to master previously intimidating tasks and challenges. What, then, is it that makes a training session effective?

Successful training requires more than just telling and expecting. Good training involves as many as of the senses as possible in as many different ways as is possible. Look back on your own education; what courses were most memorable? If you're like most of us, they are the ones that required your participation.

Engaging the senses, then, is key. In the following sections, we will discuss techniques that take advantage of the main ways adults learn best.

Seeing

We typically retain fifty percent of the information we see. Visual learning methods include videos, seminars, and live demonstrations.

Trainee programs usually start off poorly from a visual standpoint. The first thing they see is you standing behind a podium, and that, frankly, isn't very exciting. For most of us, the sight of some functionary in a three-piece suit heading determinedly down the aisle for the podium is enough to generate instant engagement of the yawning mechanism.

More effective is to start from some unconventional spot (the back of the room, for instance) and then move around the training area as you speak. Your movement will help hold the trainee's attention. If you are worried about not having your notes, there is a secret you can use: have two or three sets copied, and place them in strategic locations around the room.

Visual interest can also be generated from intelligent use of 35mm slides, overheads, and flip charts. These are all effective when they convey suddenness and a sense of urgency. There is likely to be some excitement at the revelation of a secret when a flip chart is unveiled, a slide projected, or an overhead slipped on the projector. But don't overuse these tricks! If employed sparingly, they are powerful and virtually guaranteed to lead to feverish note-taking. Overused, they can quite literally put people to sleep.

Of these mediums, 35mm slides are the most expensive and most abused. They carry another, more subtle danger: too often, poor training is hidden in the razzmatazz of powerful visuals. Slides must also be used in a darkened room which in itself can cause a certain stupor. The visual medium is there to help get the message across, not overpower or kill it.

Flip charts are good, inexpensive, and effective, but they do require that the person writing on them understands this is being done so that trainees can read the words of wisdom. Sadly, this isn't always the case. If you can't write quickly and legibly, it is perfectly acceptable to have your flip charts prepared in advance.

It is difficult to mix slides with flip charts in a given presentation (one requires darkness, the other light). Overhead projections and flip charts, however, can mix very easily and effectively. This approach provides two different visual media; add your own moving about, and you've built the foundation of a powerful and memorable training session.

You can also include training movies or videos; these, however, should as a rule of thumb never take up more than ten to fifteen percent of any training session. Training movies are an important way to power a point home, they add variety and depth, but they cannot replace a well-thought-out program.

Live demonstrations help pinpoint the differences between proficient and inadequate performance or behavior, and provide an added dimension of involvement. The more you can personalize the presentation and pull the viewer into the demonstration, the better.

Listening

We typically retain fifty percent of the information we hear. Aural learning methods include meetings, seminars, and video/audio programs.

Much of your message will come from the spoken word—on its own or though spoken word material meant to enhance visuals. Tools in this area can include films and video (the sound track) or audio programs. All are effective and can bring contrast and drama to your program.

Reading

We typically retain forty percent of the information we read. Relevant learning materials include books, manuals, and interactive audio and video programs incorporating workbooks and handouts.

Another way to change the pace and provide a mental break is to distribute handouts.

Handouts have a number of benefits. People like to get things they can take away from the training, and often begin to feel they've accomplished something once they have a piece of paper to hold. More important, handouts serve as a permanent record of the proceedings that can be used and passed on to others.

I was in Australia (a continent I had never visited) on a seminar tour recently. During a presentation, one of the attendees stopped me to show me something that would prove how closely her philosophy matched my own. What was I given? A handout from one of my own seminars conducted in the United States! If that isn't proof of the handout's superior status as a much-scrutinized, much-passed-on medium, I don't know what is.

Some trainers bind all the handouts together and give them out at the beginning of the seminar. This is a mistake, as is saving them all for distribution at the end of a program. Given away too early, the handouts will be read out of synch with your presentation, and attendees will bring up topics you don't want to address until a later point in the session. Given away too late, the handouts will resemble nothing so closely as a permanently shut book.

Distribute your handouts during the training session. You can pass them out:

- After a topic has been discussed (for reinforcement).

- Before a topic has been discussed (for use as a road-map).

Don't hand out the materials yourself if you can possibly avoid doing so; always try to get attendees to do it for you. Any involvement is good involvement!

Writing

We typically retain forty percent of the information we write. Relevant learning materials include workbooks, training forms, and written exercises.

Attendees are definitely paying attention when they are taking notes; the trick is to make it easy for them to decipher the notes later on.

Although you can't actually mandate note-taking, you can come pretty close by suppling trainees with customized workbooks. The pages of these should include headings for each of the different topics, followed by beckoning white space sufficient to accommodate all the insights that may arise.

Doing

We typically retain eighty percent of the information we accumulate through direct experience. Relevant tools include on-the-job training, real-world experience, discussion groups, and role-playing exercises.

The last two items represent the only instances where you can safely deviate from the eighteen-minute rule. Role-playing exercises and discussion groups can go on profitably for at least 45 minutes; however, unless they are carefully structured and monitored, they tend to fall apart after an hour or so. The informal discussion between participants that occurs during these exercises is tremendously valuable: it allows attendees to personalize (and perhaps even begin to implement) the topic just discussed.

Assign role-playing exercises and discussion groups to address manageable segments of your major topic of discussion. Don't try to graft the whole topic onto such exchanges; doing so will render the exercises unwieldy and ineffective. Pay particularly close attention to the instructions you give. If they are unclear or too broad, the result can be one or more of your groups sitting uncomfortably on folding chairs staring longingly at the ceiling. Beware of making the instructions too complex, as well. It is a good rule of thumb in training (indeed, for managers in general) that you can give someone up to three instructions at one time, but never more.

Evaluating the program

You can involve participants in your future program development by using implementation contracts. These are essentially carefully structured feedback sheets; a simple one will incorporate four separate areas of inquiry.

- The first will ask what the trainee found most valuable in the program.

- The second will ask how they plan to implement the new insights in their day to day activities.

- The third will ask how that person's manager can help in the efforts described in number two.

- The fourth will ask what topics would be of interest for future programs.

Trainees are asked to fill these sheets out before leaving the session. Besides helping you plan future activities, these contracts also play an important role for the program participant. Setting thoughts to paper can help crystalize ideas and turn them into commitments, and these commitments can be developed and implemented later on by the employee, acting in concert with management.

Implementation contracts can also serve to remind the employee about any commitments made over the course of the training session. The forms can be quite effective when used properly. The best technique is to wait until two weeks or so after the session, just when memory of the training is beginning to fade. It is at this point that the trainee should receive a fresh copy of the contract through office mail. In many cases, the document will serve as a powerful motivator.

TOWARD A SUPERIOR WORK FORCE

For most managers, training skills must fall into the category of "areas that need improvement." As interpersonal skills take on greater and greater importance in the workplace of the '90s, the necessity of improving these skills will become, for most of us, impossible to ignore.

The advantage to making such a commitment is that training others helps you improve the very skills you share. After all, if there is a topic you would not feel comfortable talking to others about in a training session, it is a good bet you have identified an area you could stand to review yourself!

Training is nothing less than the act of creating a superior competence where none existed before, and your ability to do so will gain you the commitment of your subordinates and superiors alike. When trainees look forward to training sessions because of the dynamic and engaging way you conduct them, the end result will be employees who emerge with confidence and commitment; employees committed to improving themselves on an ongoing basis; employees who are able to perform, and, more important, *want* to perform the things you have taught them to do.

Quick Summary of Key Concepts

- If we can justify the expense of maintaining our machines properly, we can justify the expense of maintaining our people properly.

- Many entry-level workers simply do not have the essential basic reading, writing and computational skills to serve business needs over the coming years.

- Employee training is an essential tool we will need to use more and more in the coming years.

- Good training programs can take a three-pronged approach, emphasizing:

    Straightforward skill training

    Success training

    Diversity training

- The right training for the task at hand must be preceded by the proper selection of the people to be trained.

- Many of the old, established training techniques— hours of projected slides or extensive lectures from behind a podium—do not command attention.

- Vary presentation style and encourage involvement to liven up your presentation.

Conclusion

Putting It
into Practice

So, WE MAKE THE DECISION TO CHANGE AND SUDDEN-
ly there is a whirlwind of activity. Reports, memos, and charts
issue forth; people are moved up, down, and sideways; new
positions and even departments are created, along with a slew of
task forces and special interest groups. When the dust settles,
however, things look more or less as they always did.

How can you keep it from happening? How can you work
toward long-term change?

To start with, remember that each of us can improve, at the
very least, that area for which we are responsible. By now you
should have some good ideas on how to start.

A motivating vision; steady, persistent efforts to institute a
"people-first" focus; public praise when warranted at regular
group meetings; dramatic turnarounds as a result of your work
with below-average performers; emphasis on your role as
facilitator rather than your potential as dictator; regular CPRs;
stubborn advocacy of recognition and reward for deserving
employees: all this is the stuff of which victory is made.

However impressive your own successes may be, though,
the truth is that the entire organization is not going to change unless the person at the top makes changing a top priority—and
sticks to his guns.

CHANGING THE ORGANIZATION

It's worth repeating here that keeping the best is not a one-shot affair. Those hastily composed, upbeat memos passed out to top managers won't do any harm, but they shouldn't constitute the entire strategy for reorienting a company.

The organization's top man (or woman) must see that each manager makes human resources management a primary consideration in all strategic decisions—forever. This means more than simply hearing assent to a number of broad objectives: it means being sure that one's top people feel the new agenda in their bones. The CEO will need dependable allies in this quest to make over the company from the top down, not just nodding heads. Talks, seminars, and written reminders have their place, but the only way to get the message across in a truly meaningful way is to take bolder steps.

One obvious element of this approach is to increase the perceived status of the people in the human resources department. Of course, this group is already on the ascent to some degree: many corporations have poured resources into this area to satisfy the government (that is, to accommodate the demands of legislation aimed to eradicate discrimination against women and minorities) and to give something back to society at large (that is, to pursue the noble aims of affirmative action for their own sake). Between the extremes of avoiding lawsuits and championing altruism, however, lies a more compelling reason to give the people in Human Resources high profiles: stark corporate self-interest.

The corporate leader must make the decision to include human resources people in the inner circle, because the managing of human resources has become a critical competitive concern. Prominently including HR veterans among those granted access to the corporate "holy of holies" (read: the CEO's office) will send a powerful signal throughout the organization: people matter here, and everyone should make decisions accordingly. (The general idea has been accepted widely since the end of

World War II in Europe, where the human resources department is often a road to senior management.)

If it were up to me, I would see that an HR representative sat on the board of every major company. If you think such an idea is farfetched, consider the case of Chrysler, which, verging on collapse, went so far as to put UAW chief Douglas Fraser on the board of directors as a sign of good faith to the work force during a time of dramatic restructuring. Must we face crisis, or even bankruptcy, before we undertake such initiatives?

The actual role of human resources officials at the top levels of the corporation is not the issue; what is of central importance is that the CEO find a compelling way to demonstrate his or her belief that a people-first policy makes a lot of business sense. Other approaches might include incorporating deparmental personnel developments into all managerial salary reviews, or developing departmental incentives designed to increase the sense of a team identity.

ONE DEPARTMENT AT A TIME

For those of us who aren't CEOs, the job is a little simpler, but no less important. While changing the company is a laudable long-term goal, changing one department over a shorter period is still quite an accomplishment. Your career, after all, depends on that change.

At some point, your colleagues may realize that whatever you're doing is working, and may wonder how they can duplicate your work group's achievements. Hasten that day by encouraging them to change the way they look at subordinates. Point out successful decisions you have made and sound policies you have instituted based on the three fundamental principles.

One: *The most valuable capital is human capital; the most powerful technology is people.*

Two: *A manager's success is wholly dependent upon his ability to empower others to achieve his goals.*

Three: *Great work occurs only when managers and workers share each other's visions of the present and the future.*

After all, when we create an environment where people can motivate themselves, we empower them to succeed. Their potential for success (and, therefore, our own) is unlimited.

Bibliography

Acosta, Richard: "Workplace Literacy: Let's Step on the Gas."
Delivered at the Literary Council, Rockford, Illinois, October 21,
1987. Chrysler Corporation.

Bellow, Patrick, et al.: *The Executive Guide to Strategic Planning*.
Jossey-Bass, 1989.

Baker, H.G.: "Teamwork in the Workplace." Delivered at Southeastern
Electric Exchange, New Orleans, Louisiana, April 13, 1983.
Georgia Power.

Boswell, James: "Managing Our Human Resources." Delivered at the
Newspaper Personnel Relations Relations Conference, June 23,
1986. *Los Angeles Times*.

Bowles, Lee: *No One Need Apply*. Harper & Row, 1987.

Brief, Arthur and Tomlinson, Gerald: *Managing Smart*. Lexington
Books, 1987.

Caldwell, Phillip: "Products, Prudence, People and Pride—the
Challenge to U.S. Industry." Delivered at Akron Roundtable,
Akron, Ohio, April 1, 1982. Ford Motor Company.

Carlzon, Jon: *Moments of Truth*. Ballinger, 1986.

Copeland, Lennie, and Griggs, Lewis: *Going International*. Random
House, 1985.

Copeland, Lennie, and Griggs, Lewis: *Valuing Diversity: Seven Films on American Cultural Diversity.* Copeland Griggs Productions, 1988.

Copeland, Lennie, and Griggs, Lewis: *Going International.* Copeland Griggs Productions, 1987.

Craib, Donald F.: "Communicating for Growth: A New Strategic Challenge." Delivered at Association for Corporate Growth, Chicago, Illinois, November 15, 1984. Allstate Insurance Companies.

Dahlberg, A.W.: Speech before the Institute for Certified Professional Managers, March, 1988. Southern Company Services, Incorporated.

de Michele, Mark: "Remarks on Managing and Leading People." Delivered at the Edison Electric Institute Training Directors Conference, Portland, Oregeon, August 19, 1985. Arizona Public Service Company.

Deal, Terence and Kennedy, Allan: *Corporate Cultures: The Rites and Rituals of Corporate Life.* Addison-Wesley, 1982.

Drucker, Peter: *Frontiers of Management.* Dutton, 1986.

Dunbar, Ron: "People Plus Principles Equals Performance." Delivered at Utah State University, Logan, Utah, January 23, 1985. Ryder System Inc.

Graham, Katherine: "The Glass Ceiling: Women's Barrier to Top Management." Delivered at International Women's Media Project, Washington, D.C., November 12, 1987.

Grune, George: "Shaping Our Economic Future." Delivered at Managing Directors/Advertising Conference, April 17, 1986. *Reader's Digest.*

Harrington, James: *The Improvement Process.* McGraw-Hill, 1988.

Heckert, Richard: "The Human Side of Managing Complexity." Delivered at Howard University, Washington, D.C., March 1982. E.I. du Pont de Nemours & Company.

Hickman, Craig and Silva, Michael: *Creating Excellence.* NAL, 1986.

Holder, Harold, and Odiome, George: Speech before the ANPA Labor and Personnel Relations Conference, January, 1987. American Newspaper Publishers Association.

Jacob, John: "Remarks on Affirmative Action." Delivered at Conference on Equal Employment Opportunity and Affirmative Action, Atlanta, Georgia, March 3, 1983. National Urban League.

Johnson, C.W.: "Meeting Technology and Human Resources Needs through University and Industry Interface." Delivered at Howard University, Washington, D.C., April 11, 1985. Honeywell, Inc.

Johnson, John F.: Speech before the Management Policy Council, October, 1982. Lamalie Associates.

Kearns, David: Speech before the University of Chicago Graduate School of Business, April 8, 1986. Xerox Corporation.

Kellogg, Marion: "Thoughts on the Key Relationship of Human Resources Technology to the Bottom Line." Delivered at International Human Resources Conference, September 22, 1983. Emhart Corporation.

Kidon, Robert: "A Manufacturer's View of the Socioeconomic Transformation—Its Impact on the Workplace." Delivered at Center for Urban Community Development, Milwaukee, Wisconsin, November 30, 1983. Rexnord, Incorporated.

Kizer, William: "Creating the Healthy Workplace." Delivered at Corporate Wellness Fair, Milwaukee, Wisconsin, May 21, 1987. Central States Health And Life.

Kizer, William: *The Healthy Workplace: A Blueprint for Corporate Action*. John Wiley, 1987.

Korell, Don: "Planning for the Future Office—Today." Delivered at Ergo-Design Conference, November 8, 1984. Steelcase, Inc.

Korn, Lester: "The 21st Century: The Era of the Megamanager." Delivered at Town Hall of California, Los Angeles, June 3, 1986. Korn/Ferry International.

Levering, Robert: *The 100 Best Companies to Work For in America*. NAL, 1987.

Levinson, Daniel: *Seasons of a Man's Life*. Knopf, 1978.

Lutz, Robert: "Rethinking Productivity—A Wholistic Apprach." Delivered at the University of California at Los Angeles, November 4, 1982. Ford Motor Company.

Maccoby, Michael: *Why Work*. Simon & Schuster, 1987.

Morita, Akio: *Made in Japan*. NAL, 1988.

Morrison, Peter: "Demographic Surprises Ahead—Blind Spot in Your Corporation's Planning?" Delivered at Town Hall of California, Los Angeles, July 23, 1982. Rand Corporation.

Naisbitt, John and Aburdene, Patricia: *Reinventing the Corporation*. Warner Books, 1985.

Navarro, Antonio: "Hispanics and Corporate America." Delivered at Southeast Bank Conference, Miami, Florida, October 1, 1986. W.R. Grace & Co.

Nelton, Sharon: "Meet Your New Workforce." *Nation's Business*, July, 1988.

Office of the Secretary of Labor: Women's Bureau newsletters and publications, 1985-1989. United States Department of Labor.

Ong, John D.: "Workplace 2000: Managing Change." Delivered at National Alliance of Business Conference, Atlanta, Georgia, March 25, 1988. B.F. Goodrich Company.

Peters, Tom: *Thriving on Chaos*. Harper & Row, 1988.

Peters, Tom and Waterman, Robert: *In Search of Excellence*. Warner Books, 1984.

Pinchot, Gifford: *Intrapreneuring*. Harper & Row, 1985.

Pryor, Fred: *The Energetic Manager*. Prentice-Hall, 1987.

Renier, J.J.: "Work Ethic—Or Employment Ethics?" Delivered at Town Hall of California, Los Angeles, October 4, 1982. Honeywell, Incorporated.

Renner, William B.: "Corporate Culture." Delivered at Blount Chamber of Commerce, Maryville College, Maryville, Tennessee, February 18, 1982. Aluminum Company of America.

Roberts, Roy: "Change and the Importance of People." Delivered at the University of Michigan, Detroit, Michigan, November 13, 1987. General Motors Corporation.

Roethlisberger, F.S.: *Management and Morale*. Harvard University Press, 1941.

Rolland, Ian: "The Human Equation in the New Corporation." Delivered at Town Hall of California, Los Angeles, September 21, 1982. Lincoln National Insurance Company.

Rubin, Theodore: *Overcoming Obstacles*. Harper & Row, 1985.

Rungan, Marvin: Speech before the Economic Club of Detroit, February, 1986. Nissan Motors Manufacturing Corporation in U.S.A.

Schumer, Allen: "Employee Involvement." Delivered at Association for Quality and Participation Conference, Indianapolis, Indiana, April 14, 1988. Miller Brewing Company.

Scott, Peter: "Beyond the Bottom Line: A CEO's Vision." Delivered at Senior Management Conference, Williamsburg, Virginia, June 1987. Emhart Corporation.

Shapiro, Albert: *Managing Professional People*. Free Press, 1985.

Sherman, Clayton: *From Losers to Winners*. Amacom, 1987.

Silva, Michael, et al.: *The Future 500*. NAL, 1987.

Skivington, James: *Managing to Survive*. Sterling, 1988.

Smith, Roger: Speech given at the University of Chicago Graduate School of Business, April 8, 1987. General Motors Corporation.

Smith, Roger: Speech before the Health Insurance Corporation, Omaha, Nebraska, June 16, 1986. General Motors Corporation.

Smyth, H. Gordon: "Motivating Employees During a Period of Downsizing." Delivered at Annual Human Resources Conference, October 24, 1986. E.I. du Pont de Nemours & Company.

Smyth, H. Gordon: "Changes in the Employee Relations Field." Delivered at Rotary Club, Tryon, North Carolina, March 3, 1986. Dupont Corporation.

Stempel, Robert: Speech before the Conference on the Aging Workforce, Detroit, Michigan, March 10, 1988. General Motors Corporation.

Thacher, Ken: Empowerment and Bureaucracy. *Training and Development Journal*, September, 1988.

Tomasko, Robert: *Downsizing*. Amacom, 1987.

Watton, Mary: *The Deming Management Method*. Dodd, Mead, 1986.

Welch, John: "Managing for the Nineties." Delivered at annual shareholder's meeting, Waukesha, Wisconsin, April 27, 1988. General Electric Corporation.

Index

If you have any comments or suggestions on the topics covered in this book, do not hesitate to contact me.

Please send your comments and suggestions to:

Martin Yate
c/o Bob Adams, Inc.
260 Center Street
Holbrook, MA 02343